# FLOWER COLORING BOOK

## LARGE PRINT

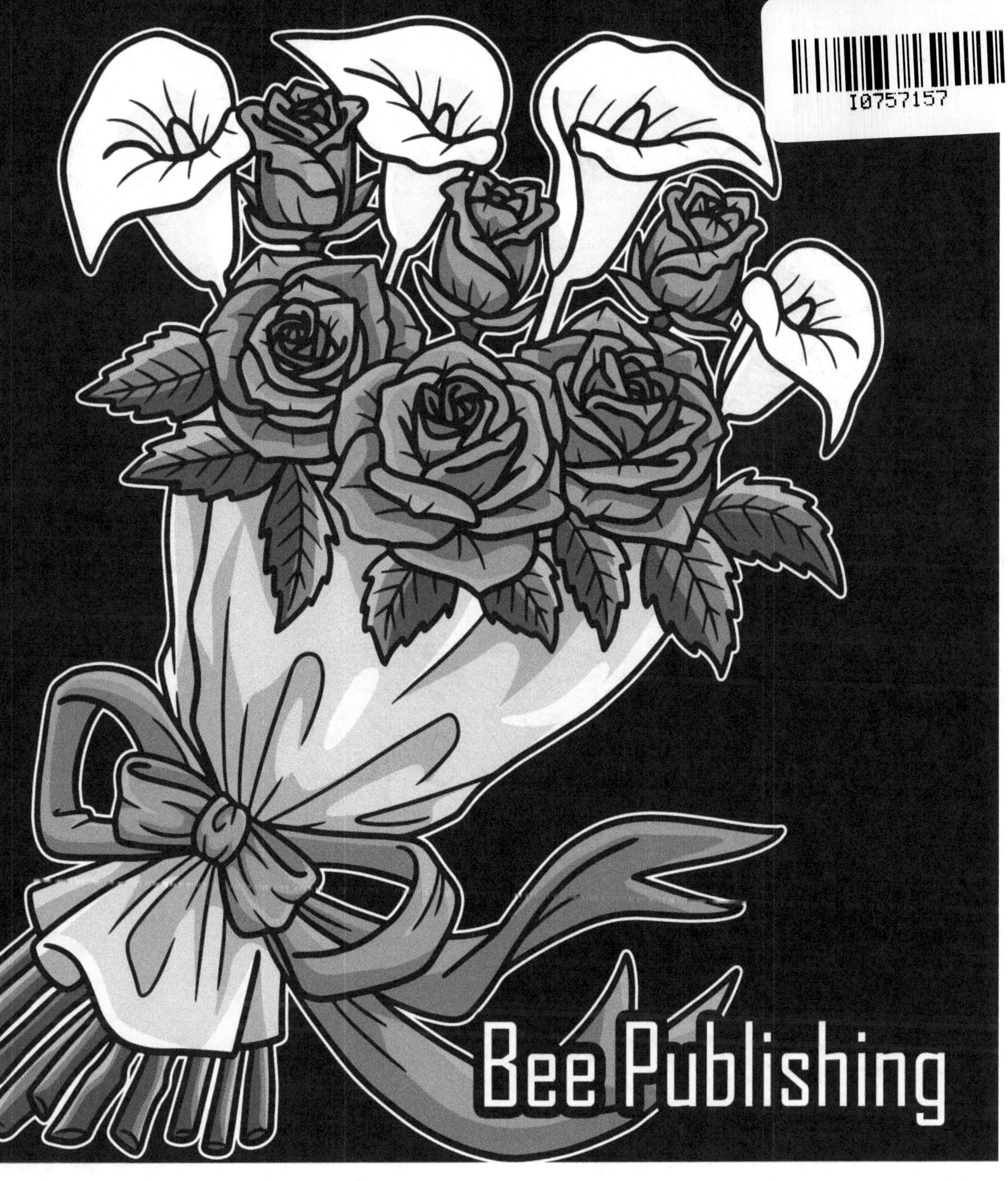

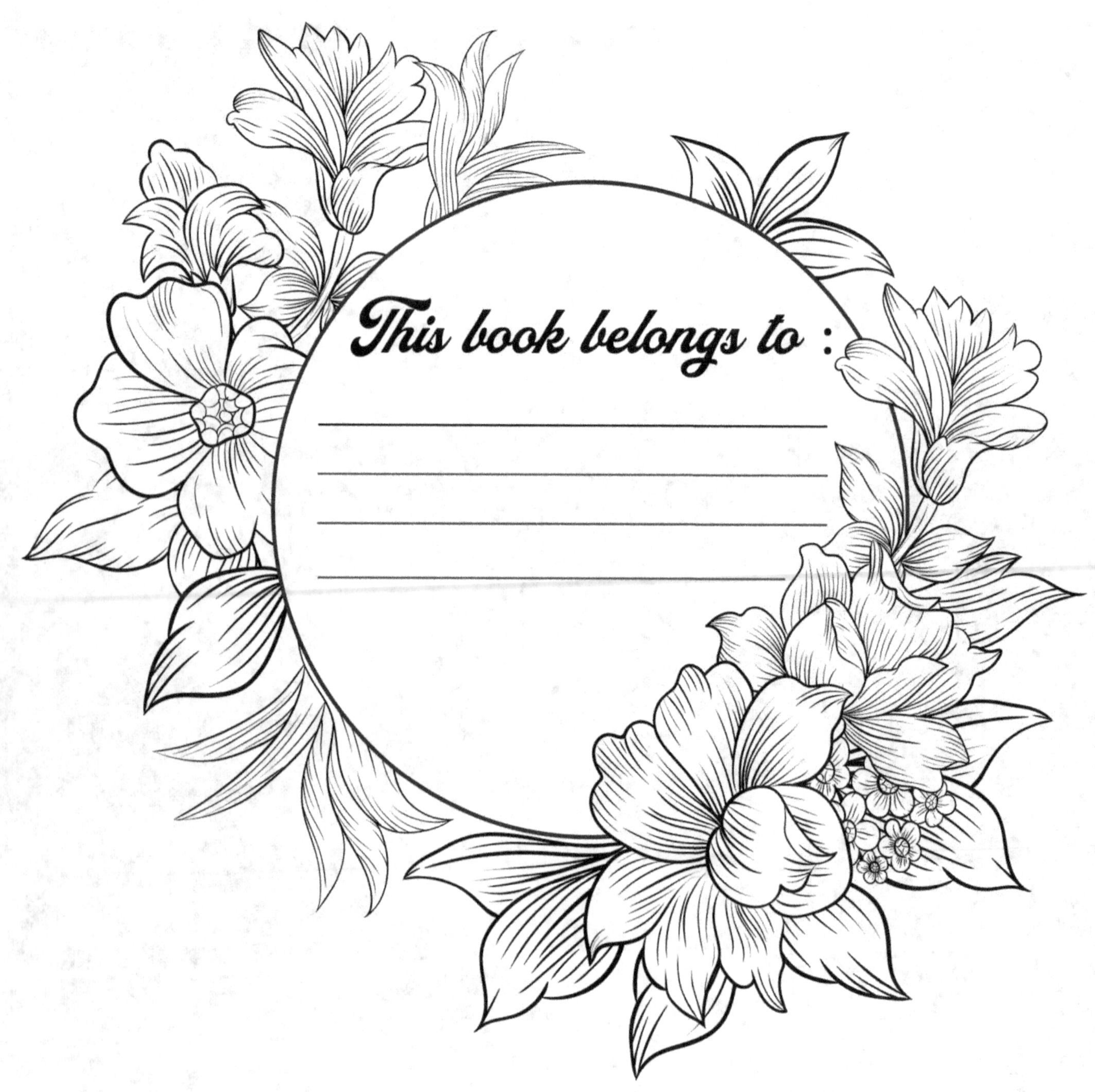
This book belongs to :

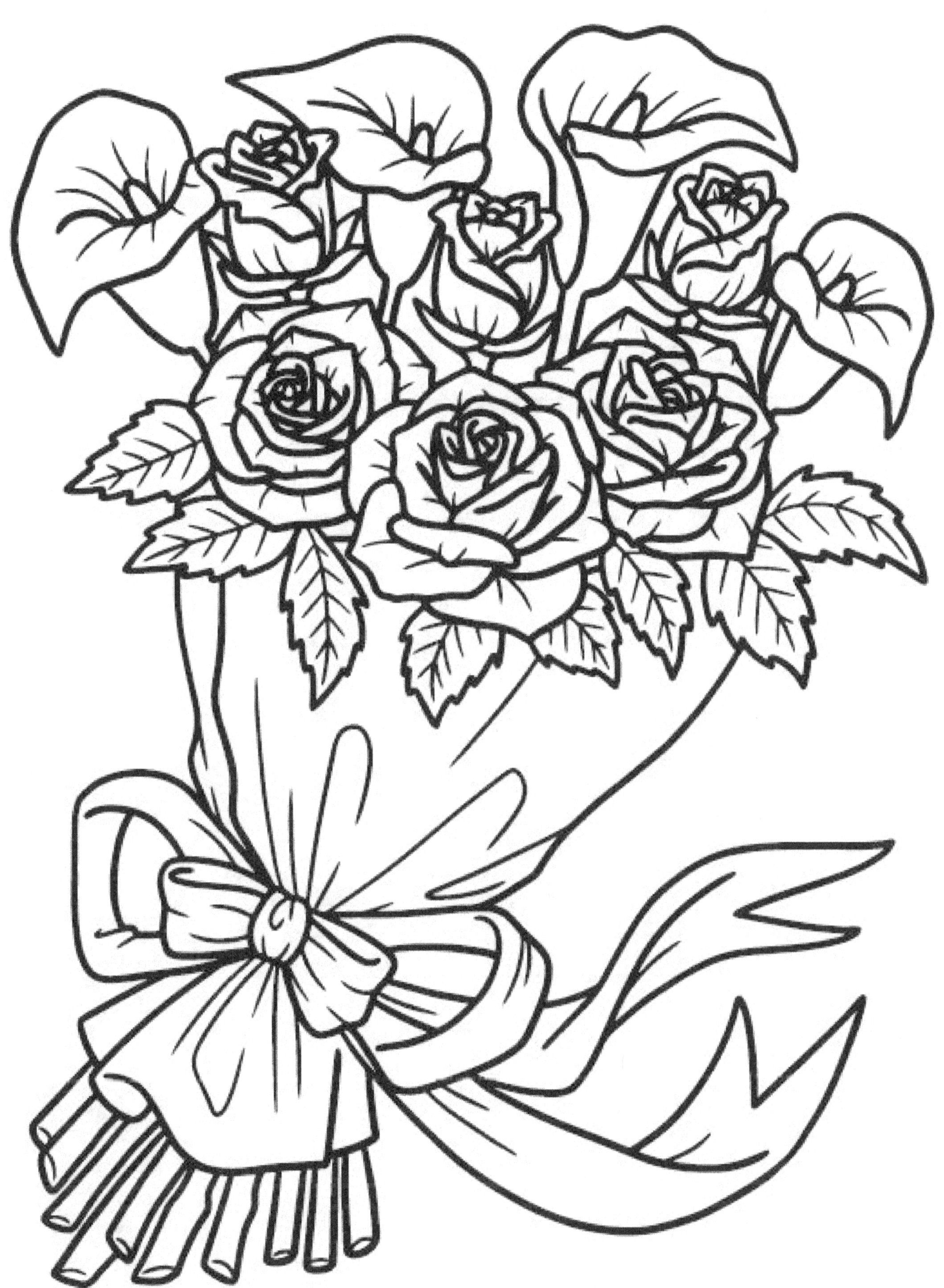

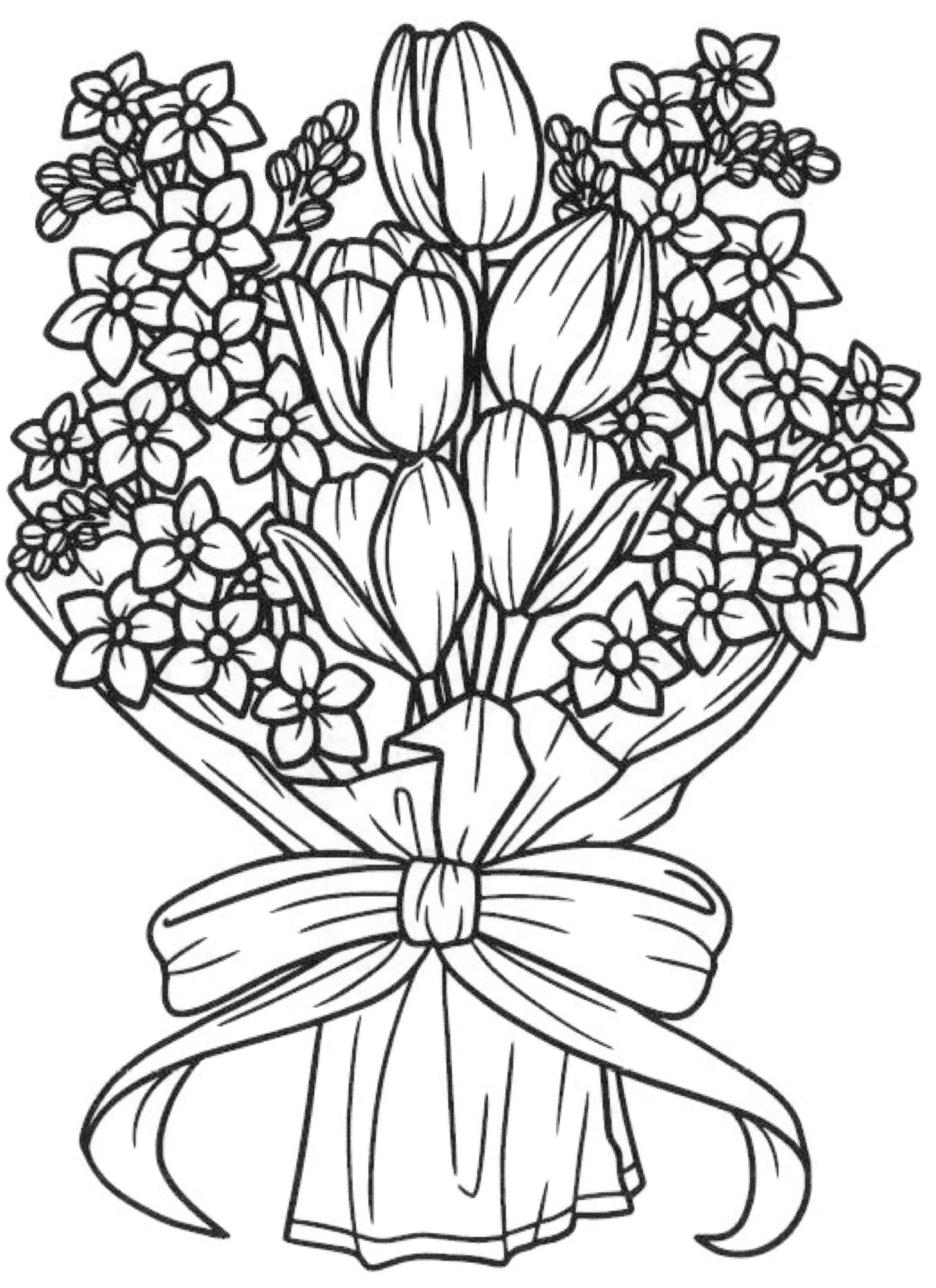

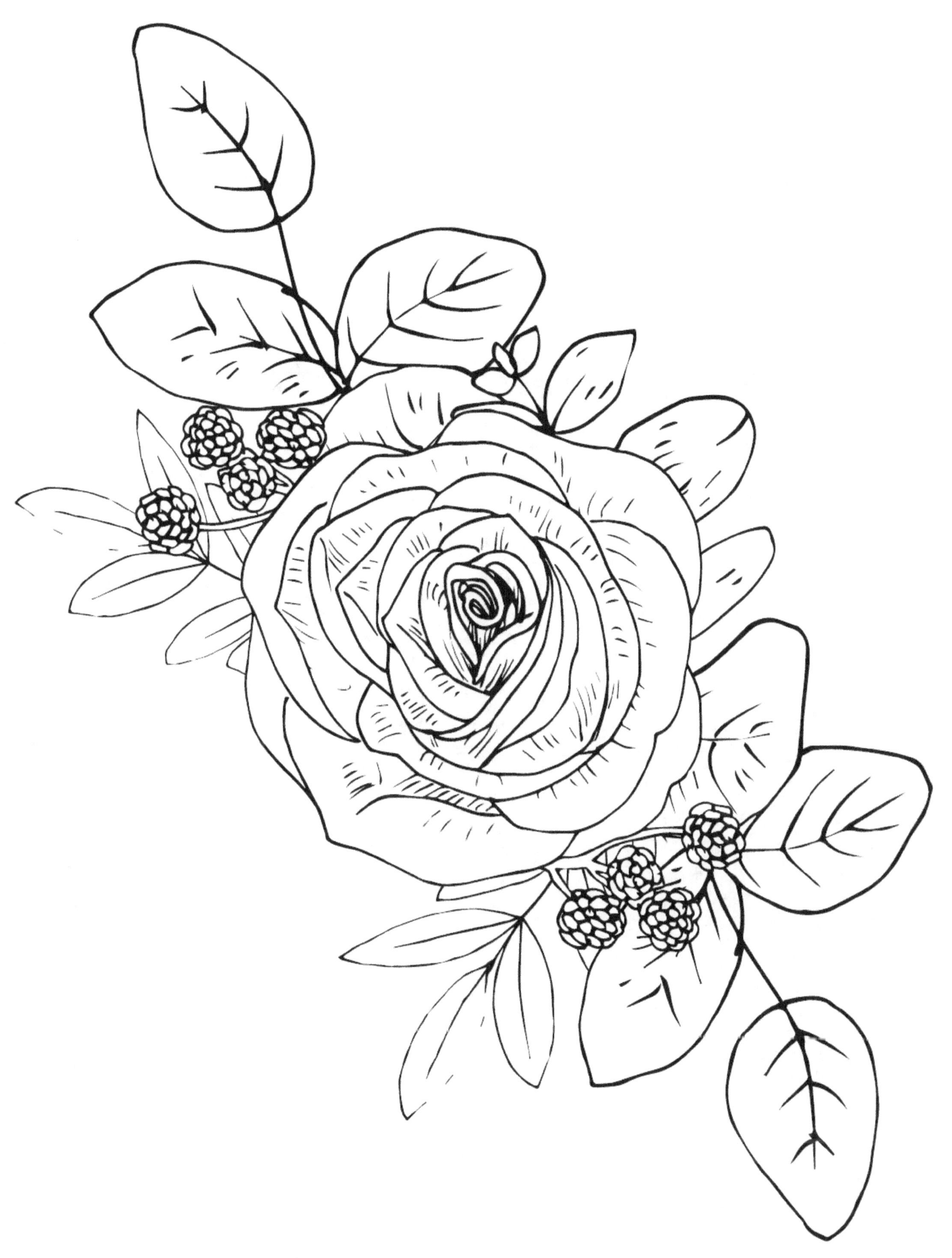

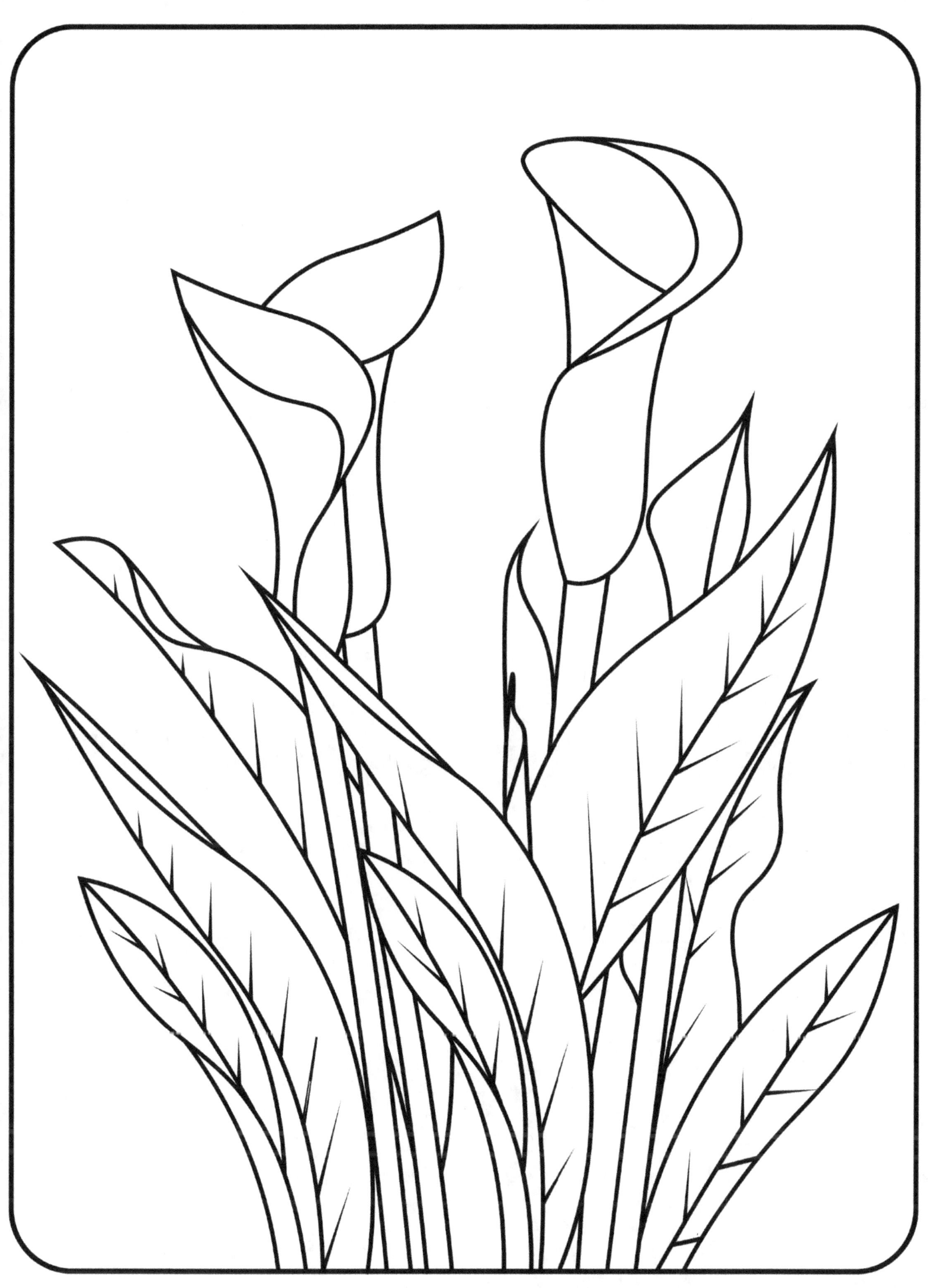

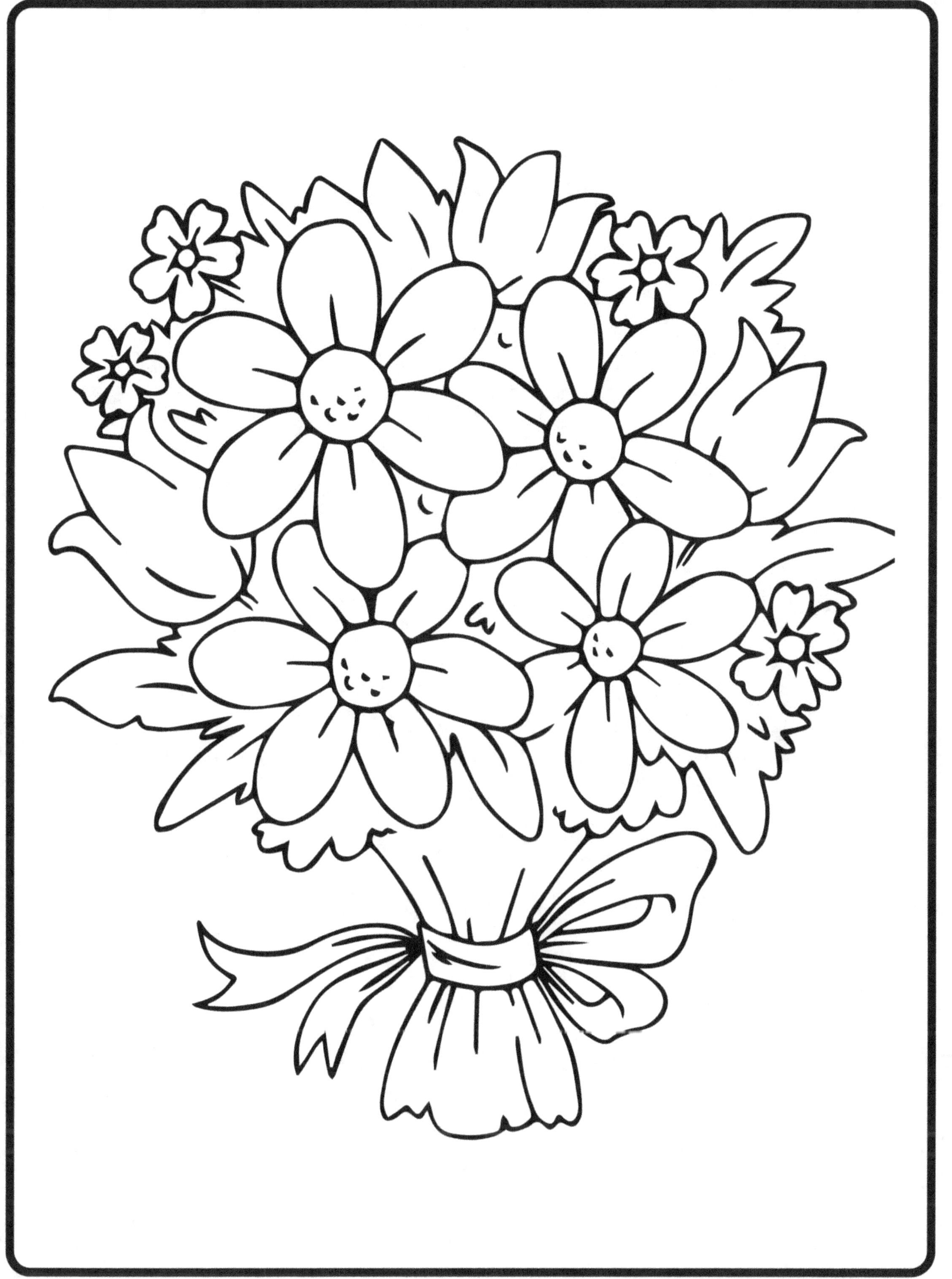

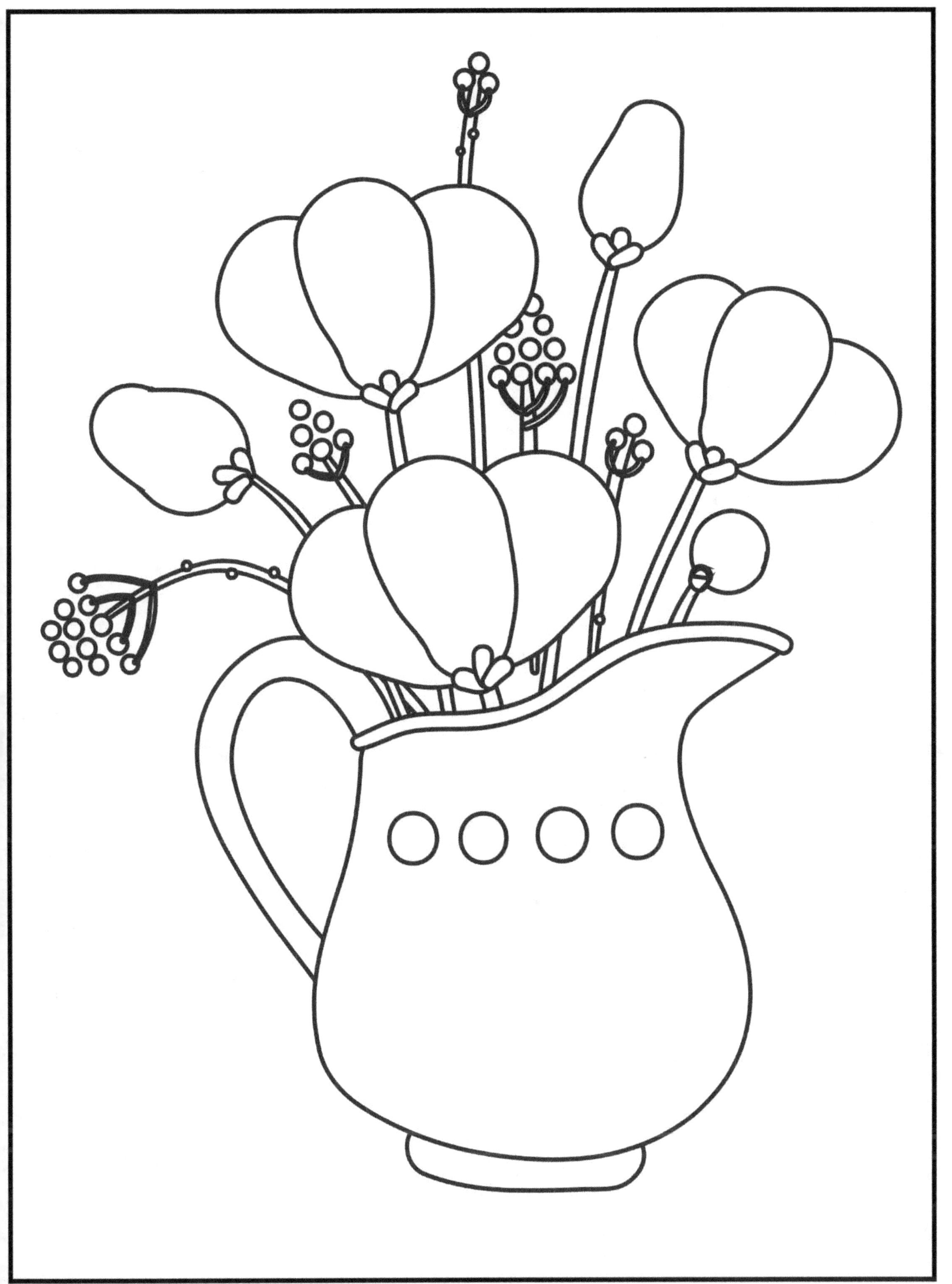

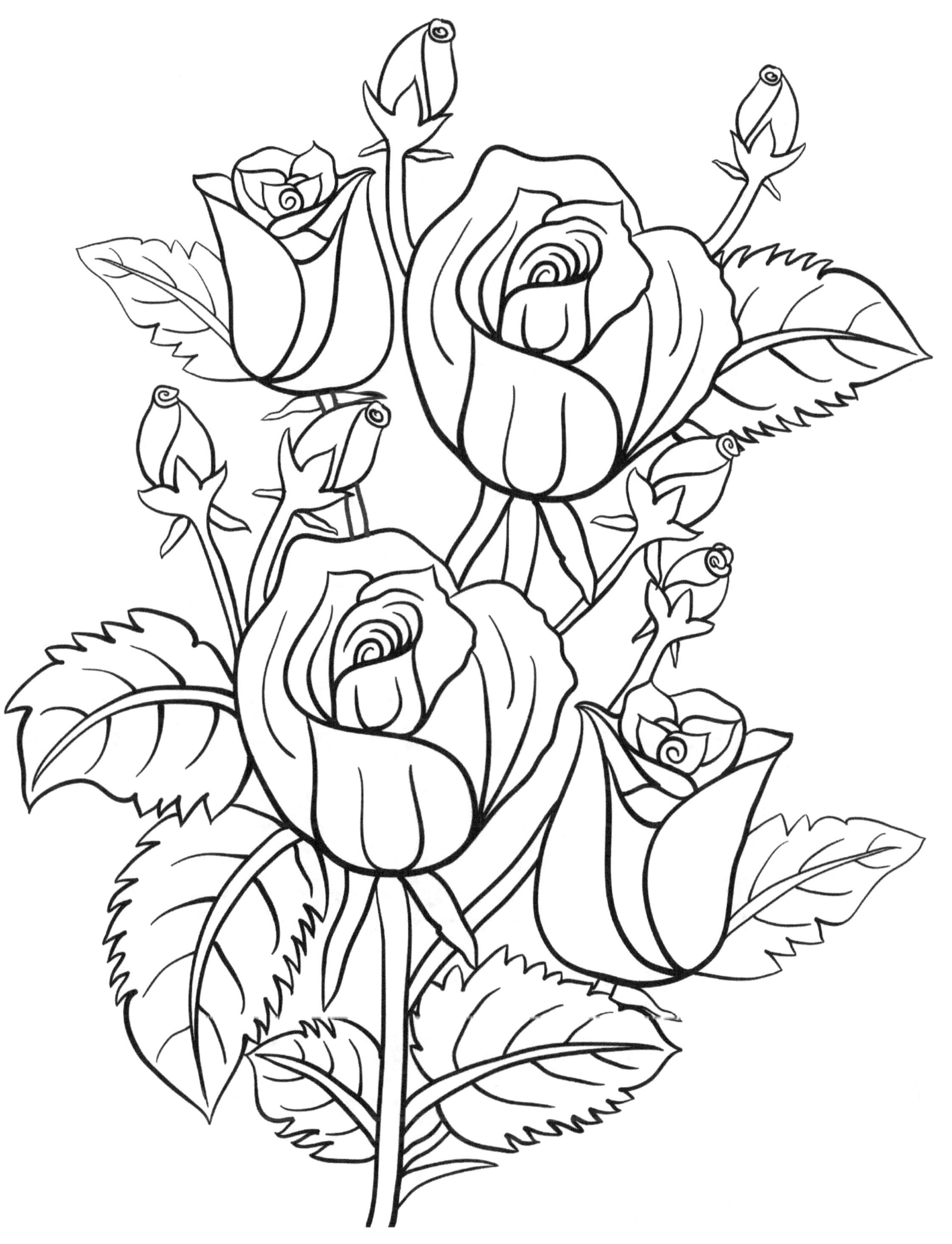

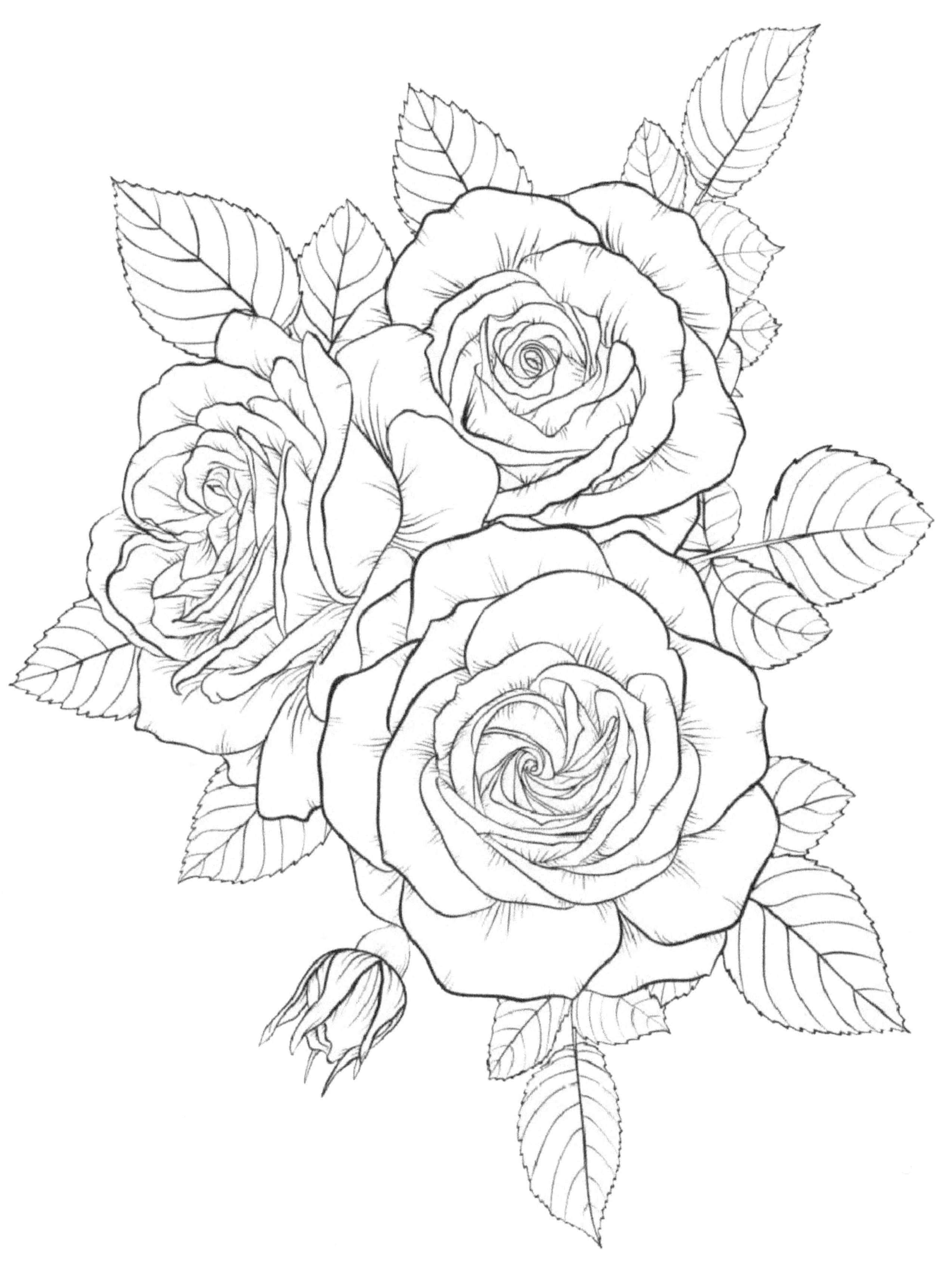

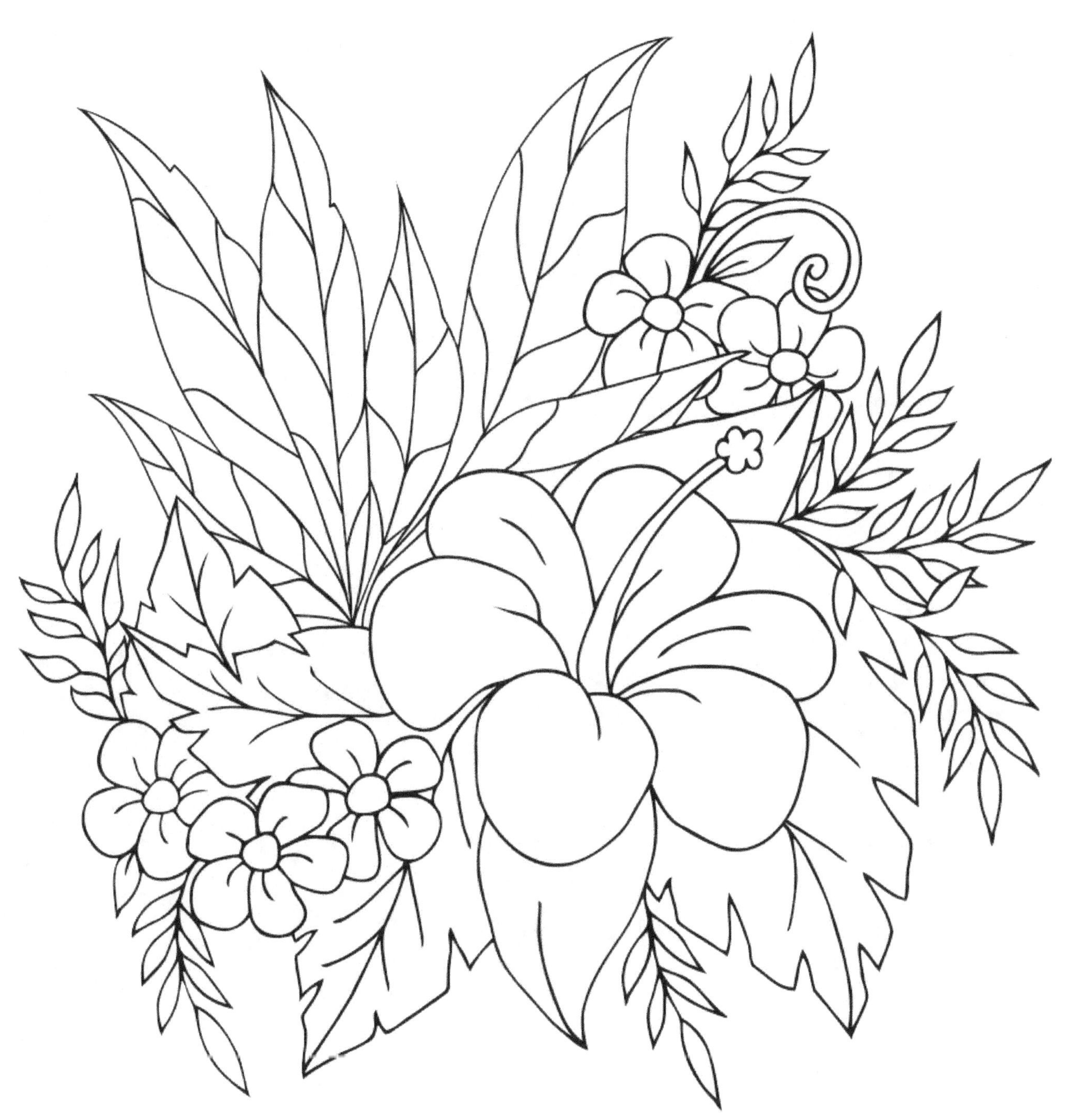

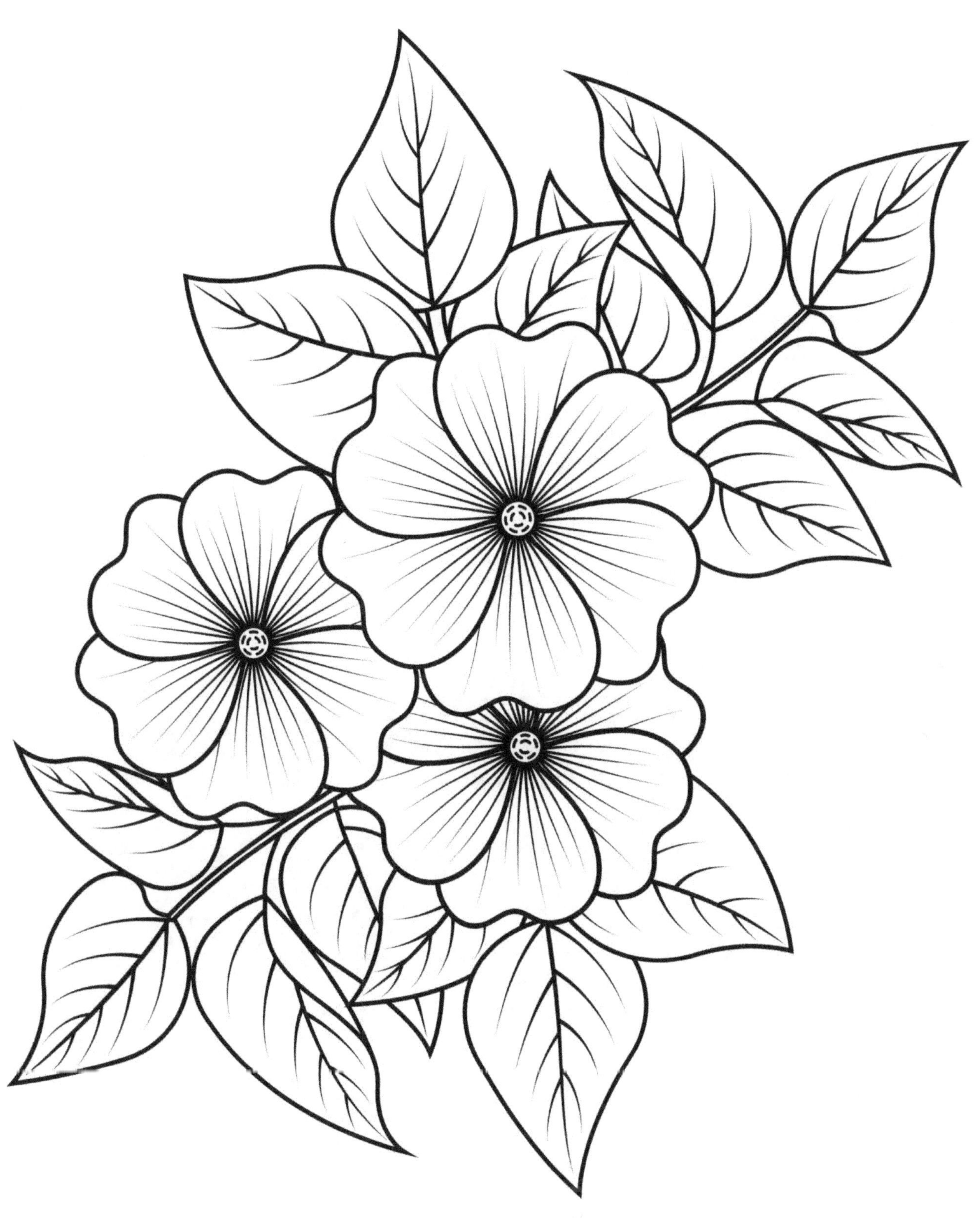

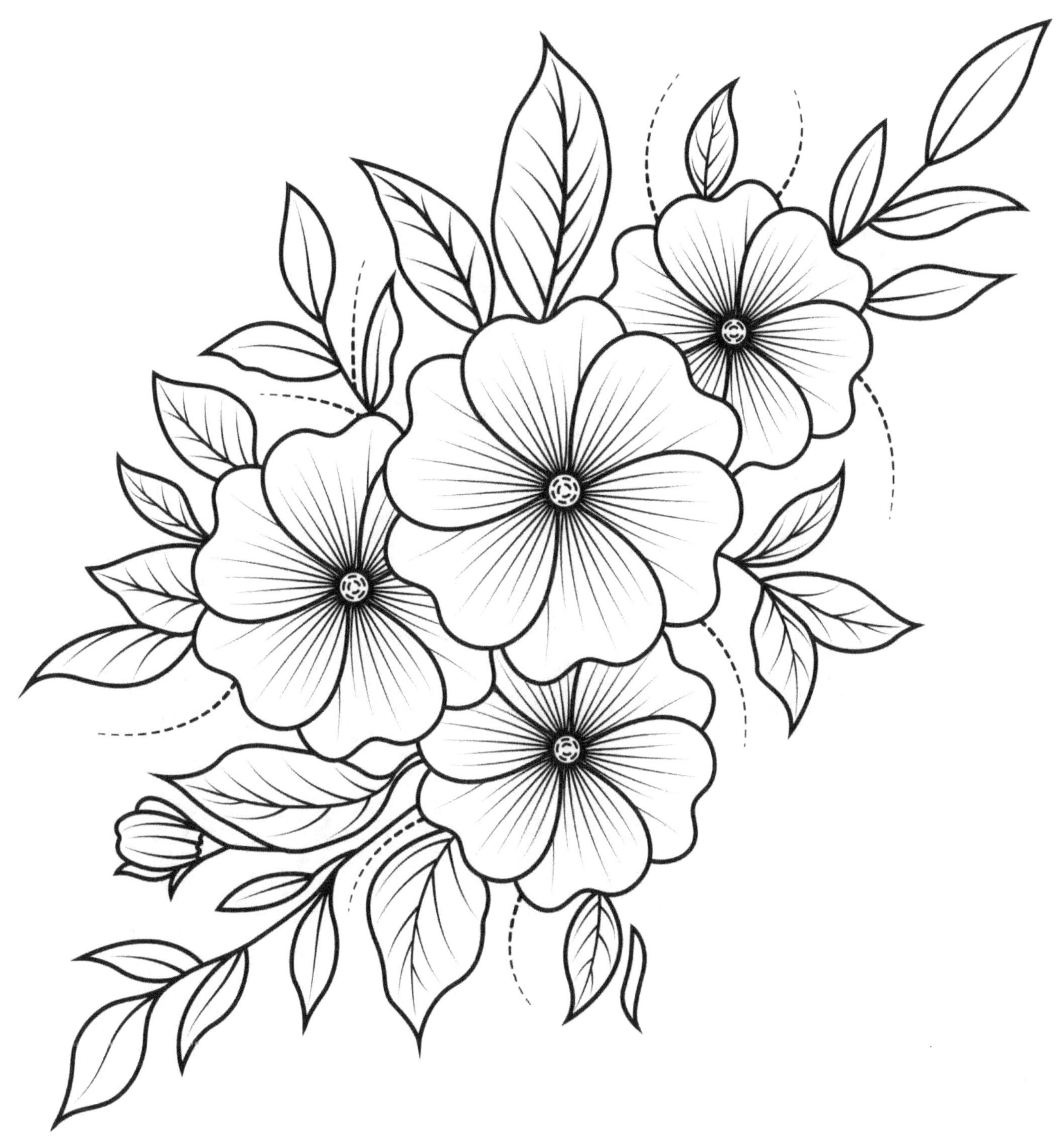

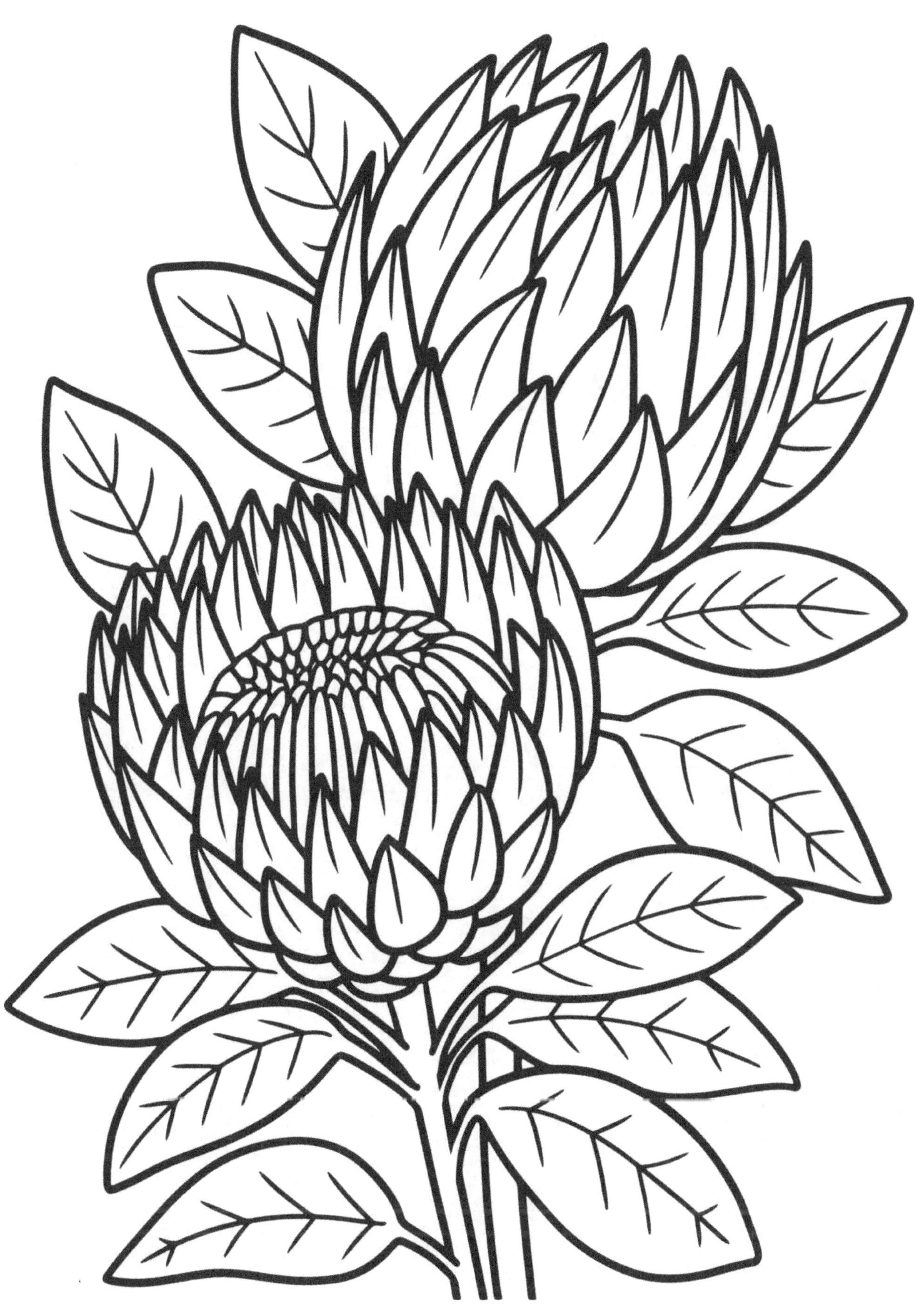

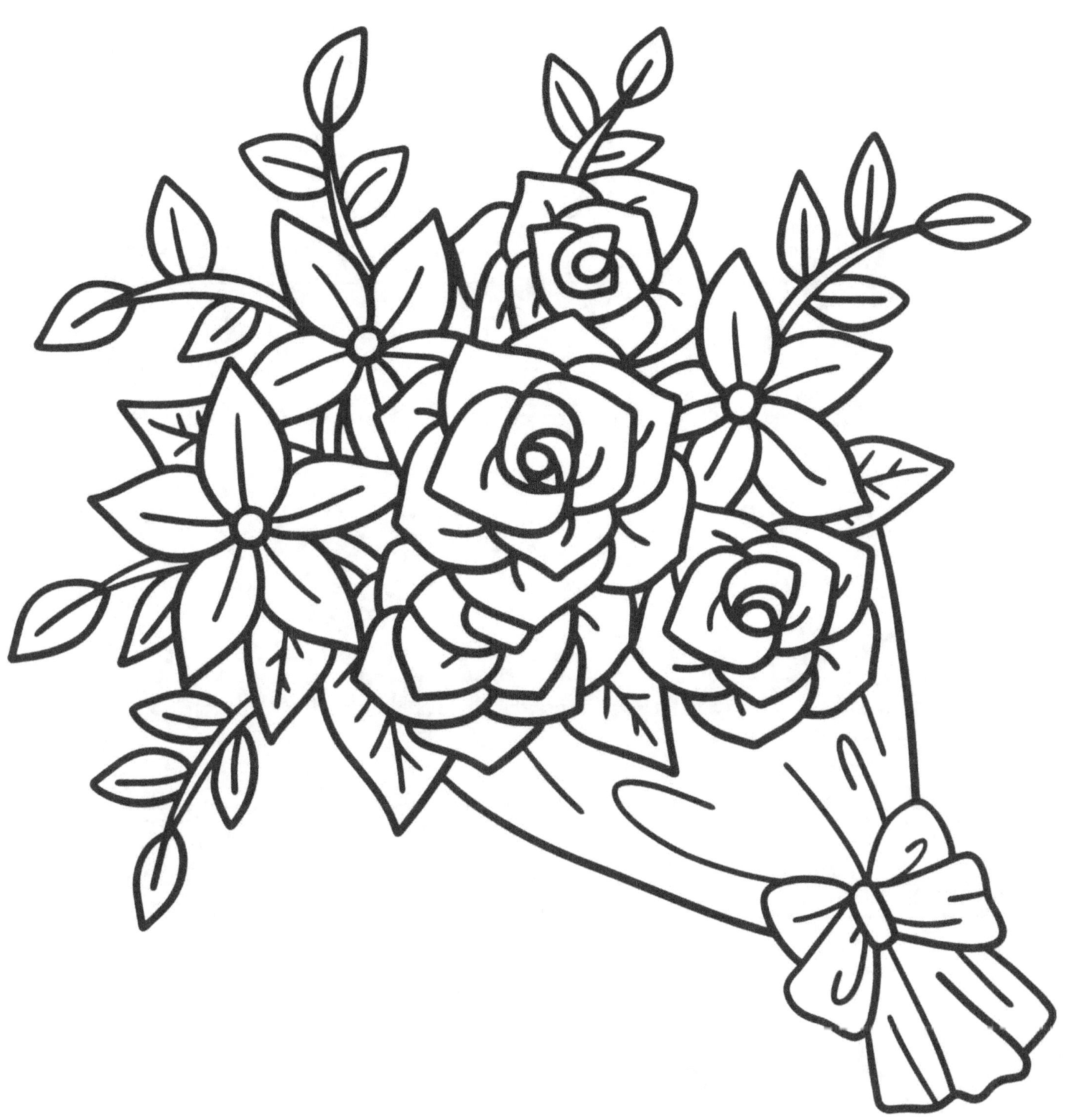

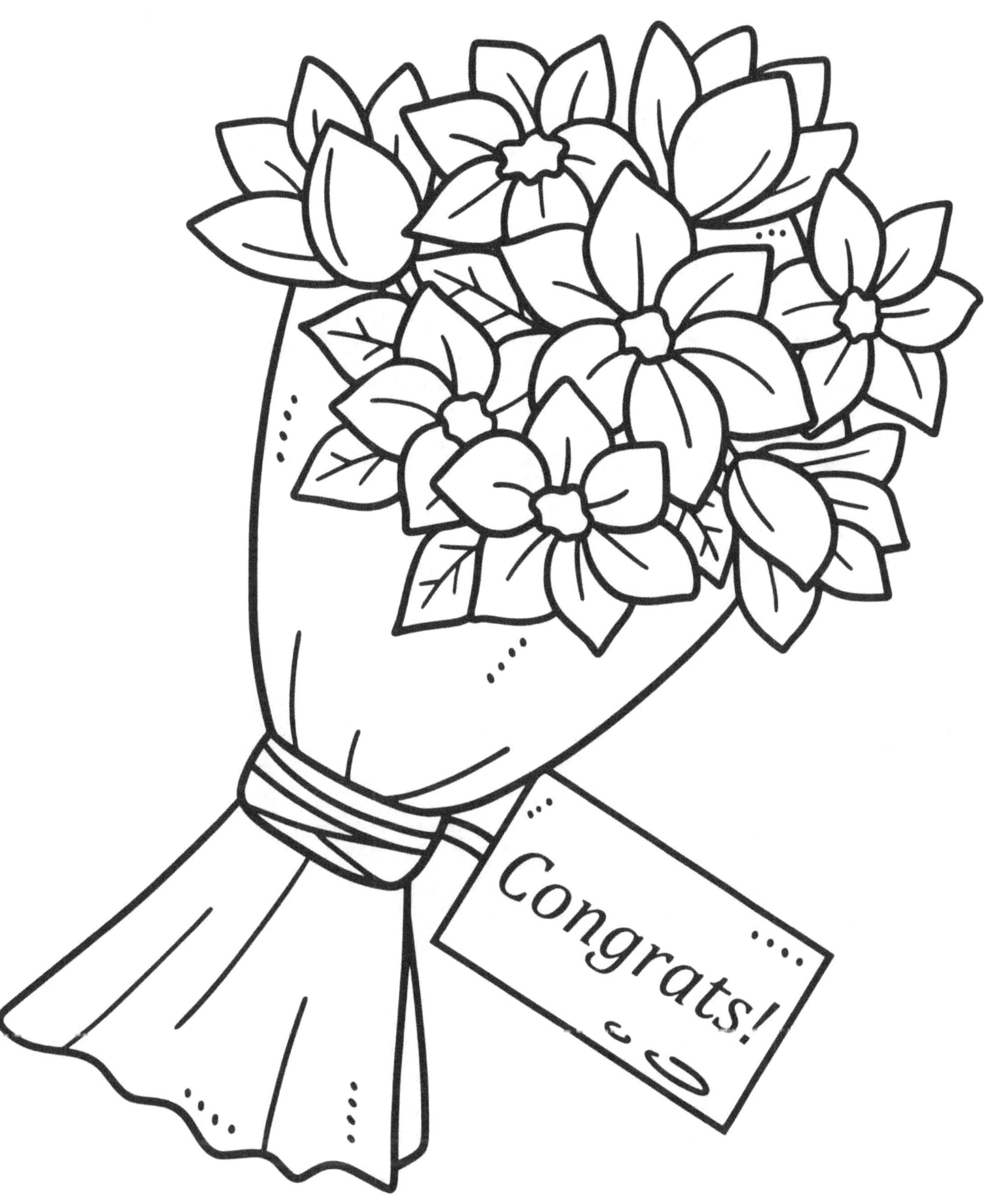
Congrats!

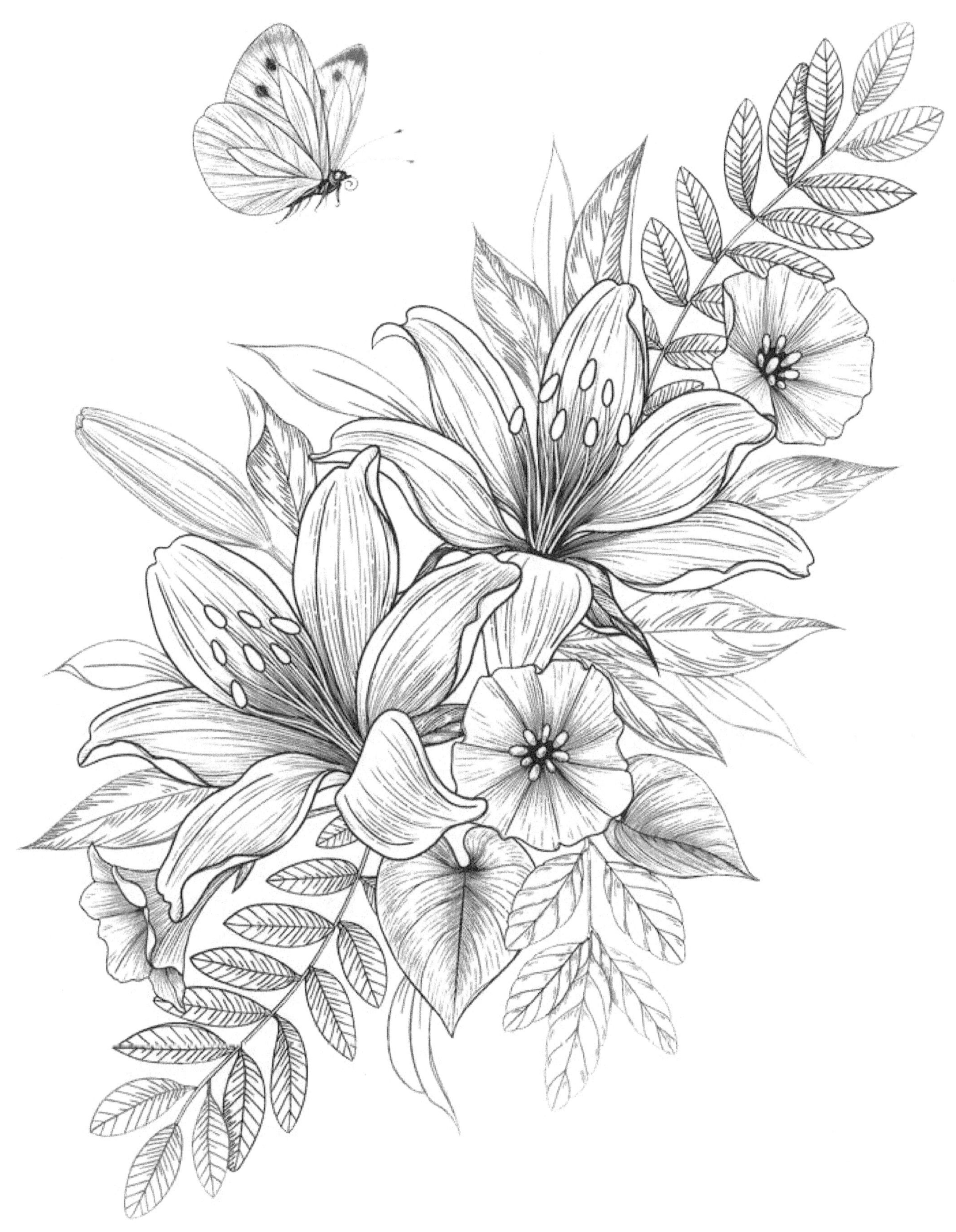

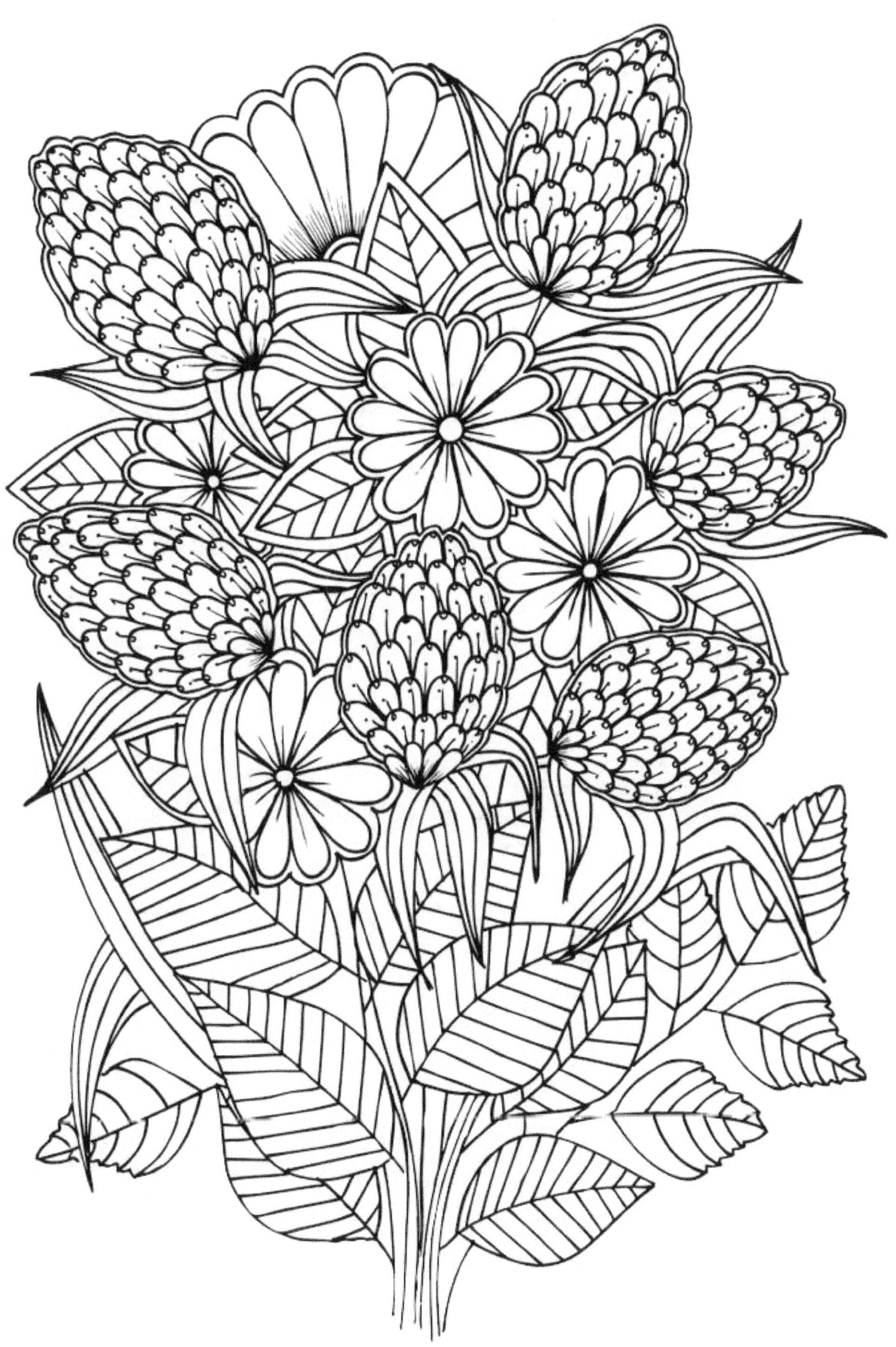

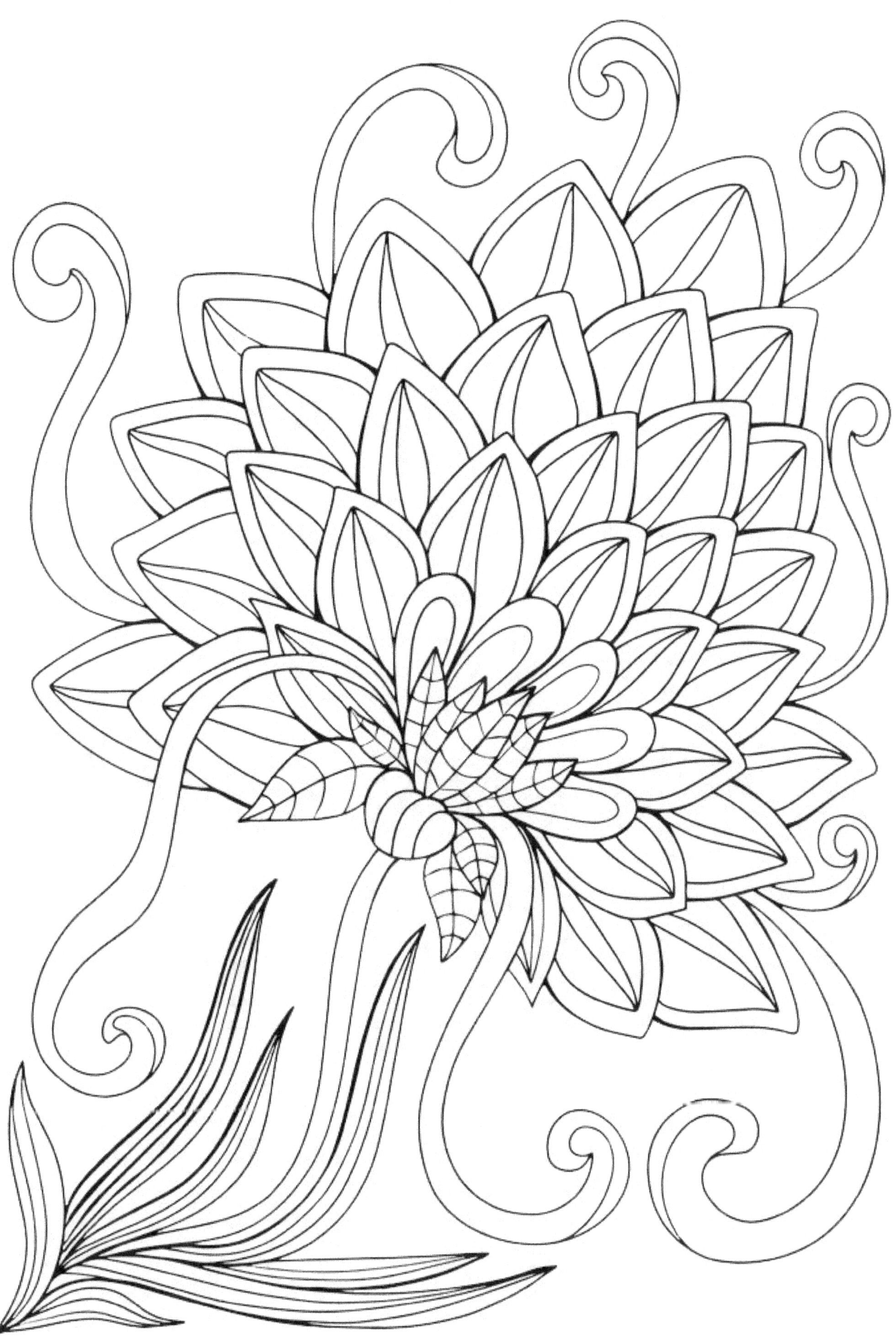

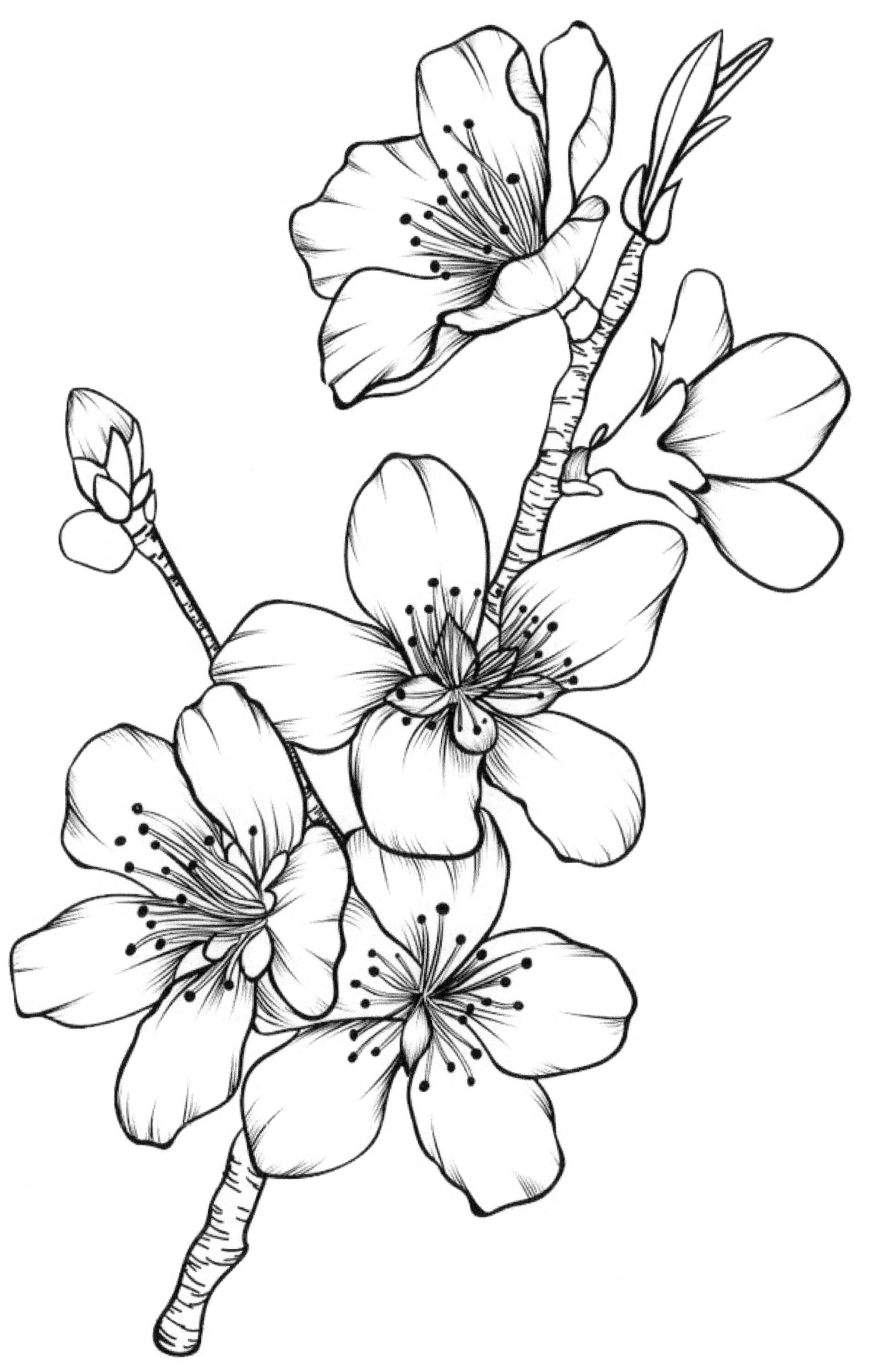

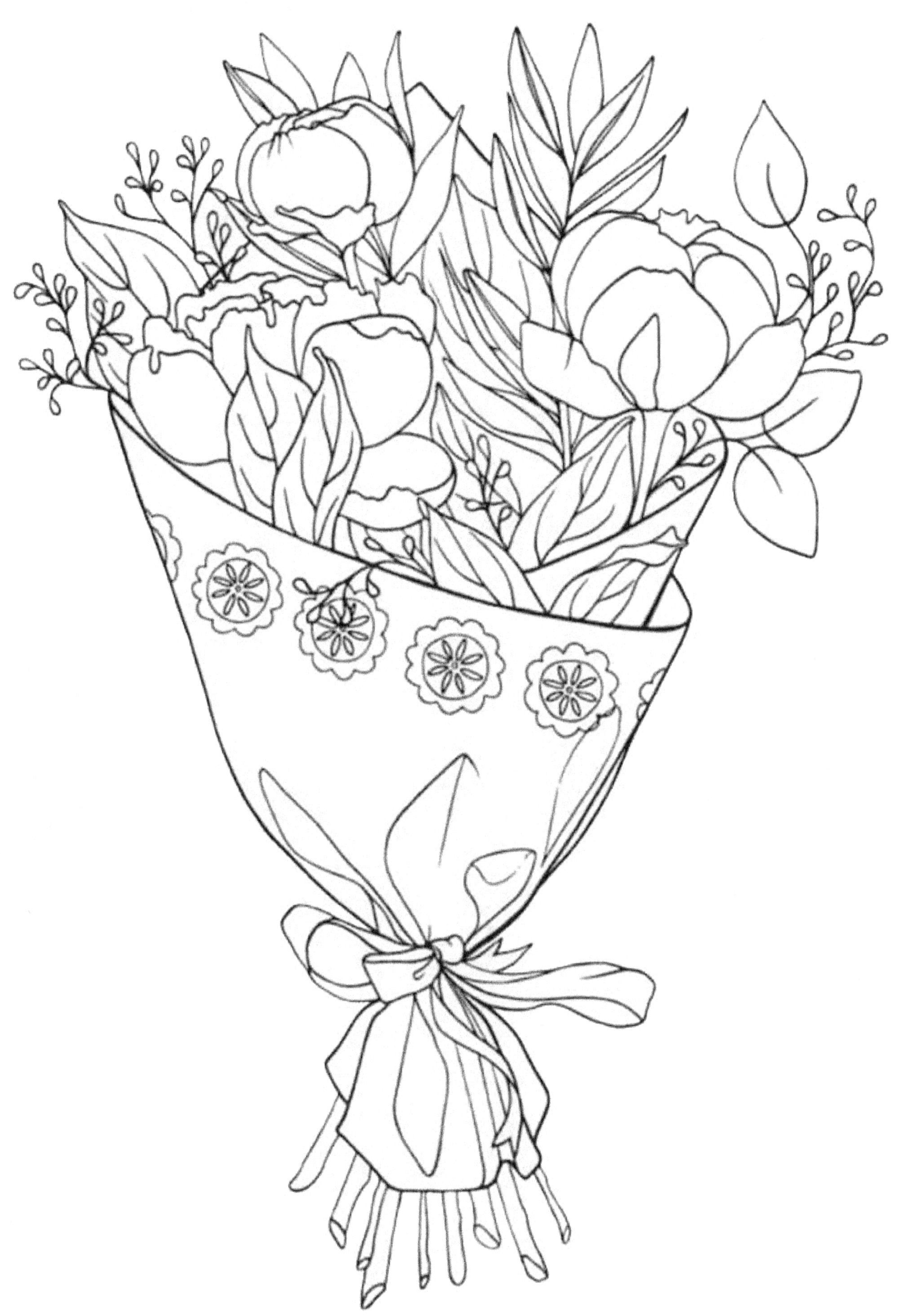

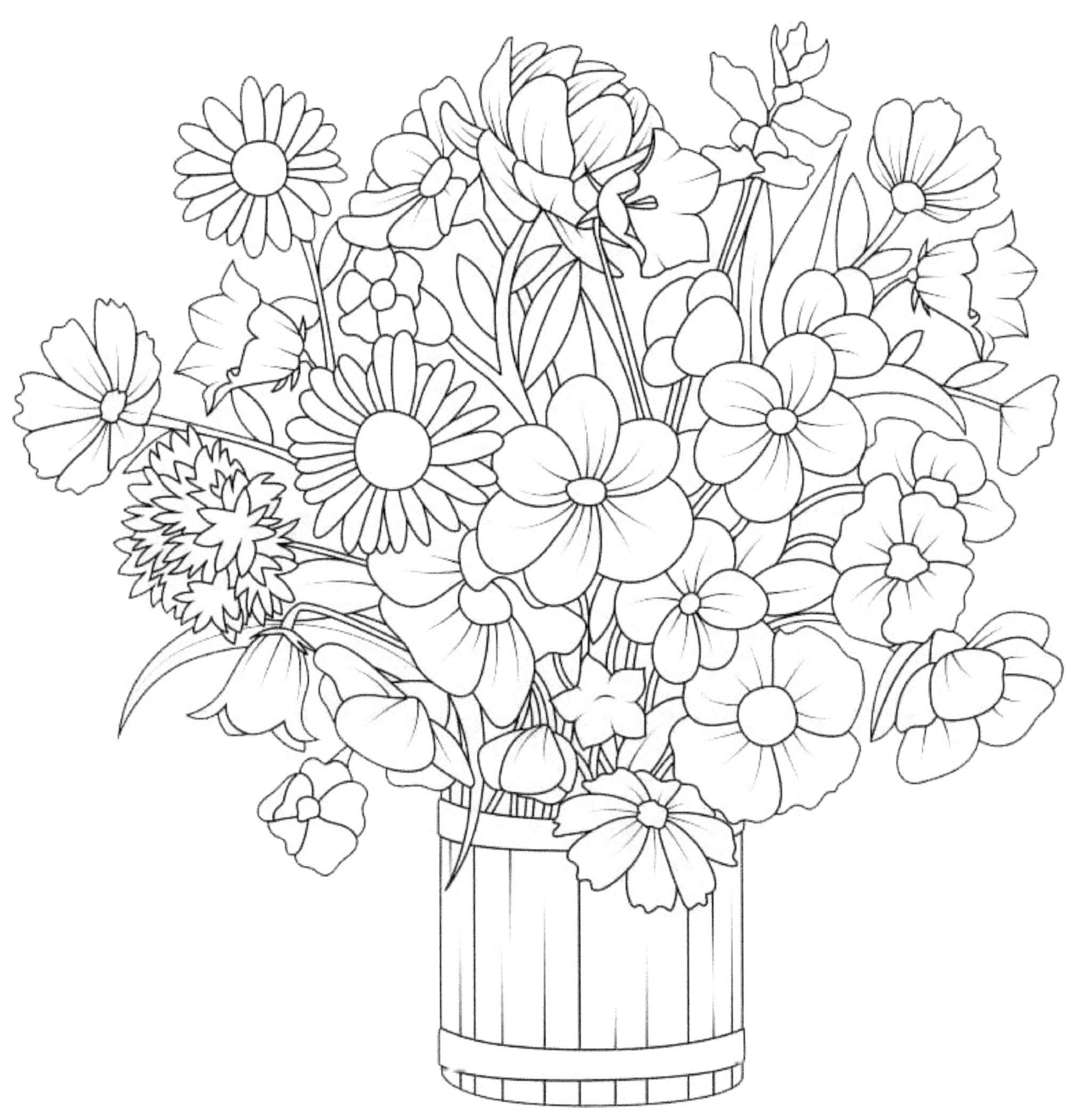

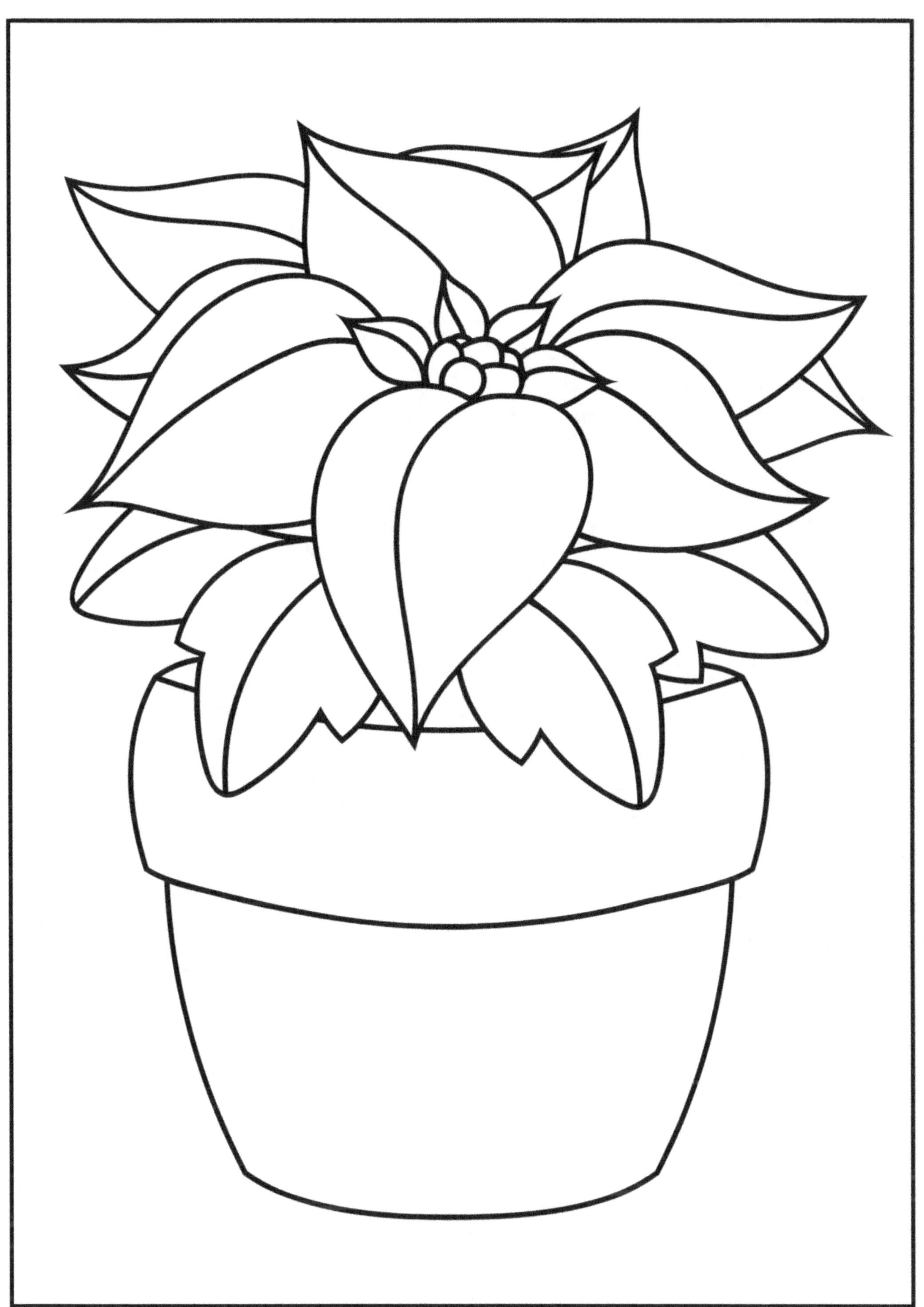

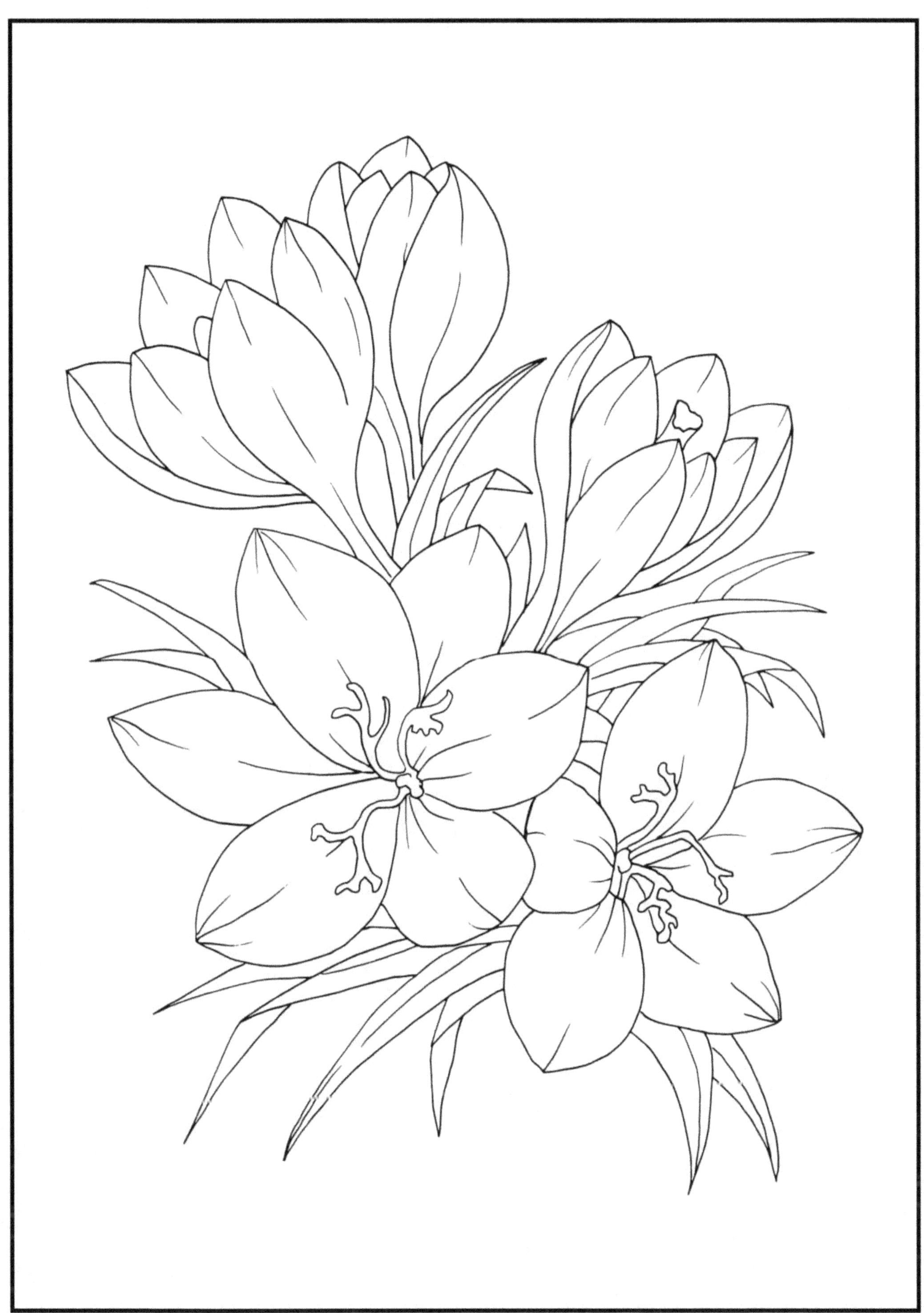

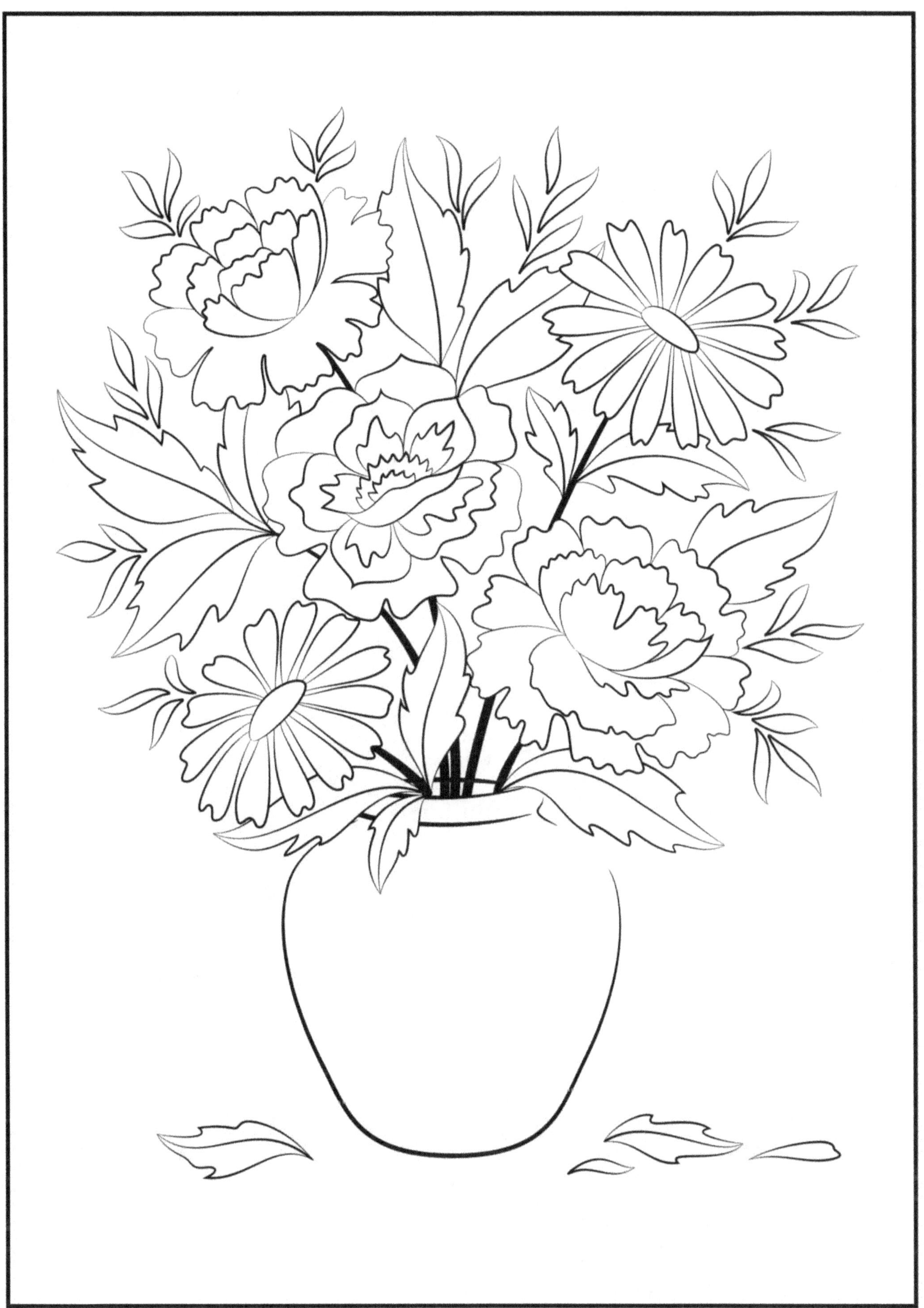

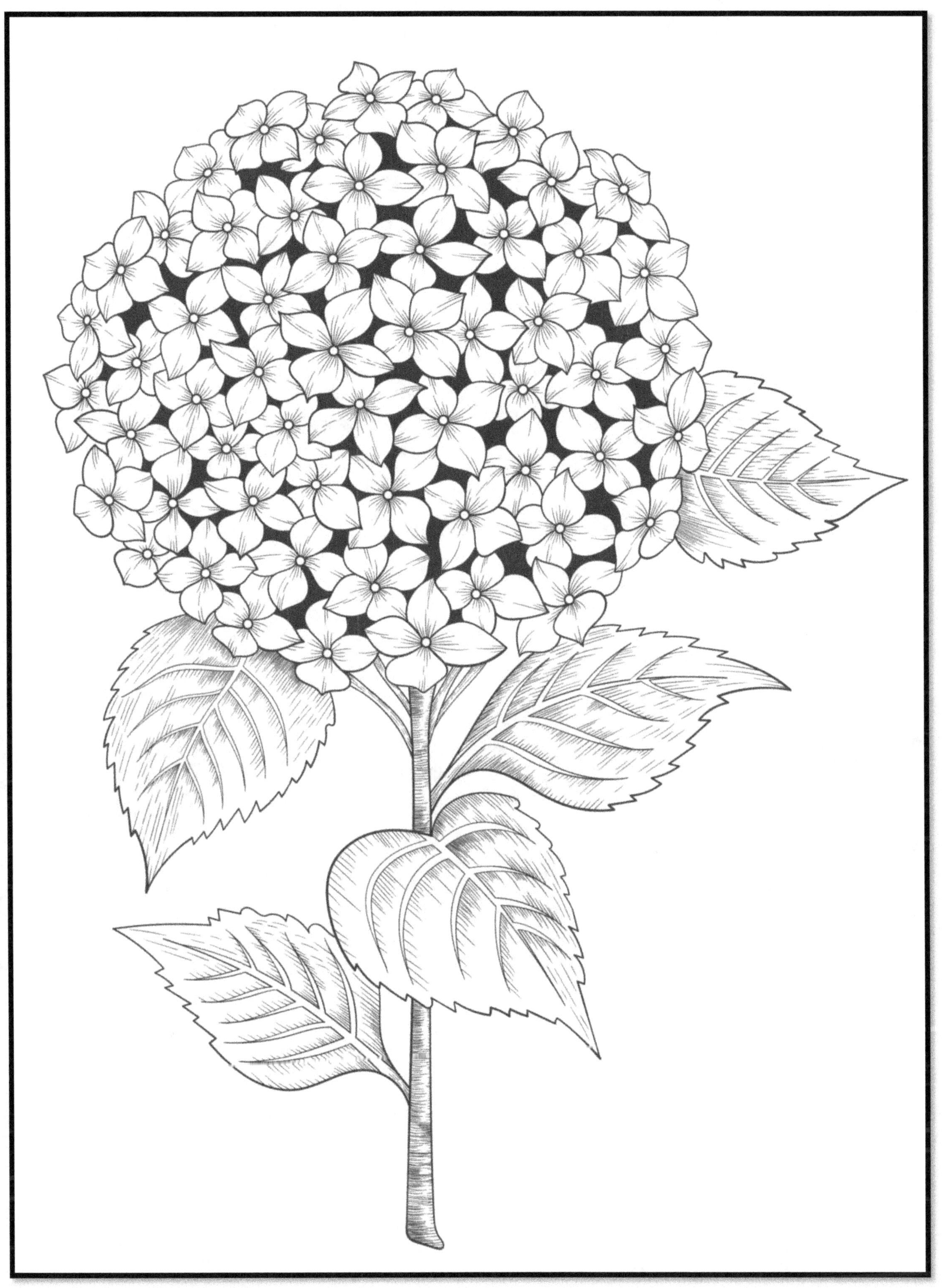

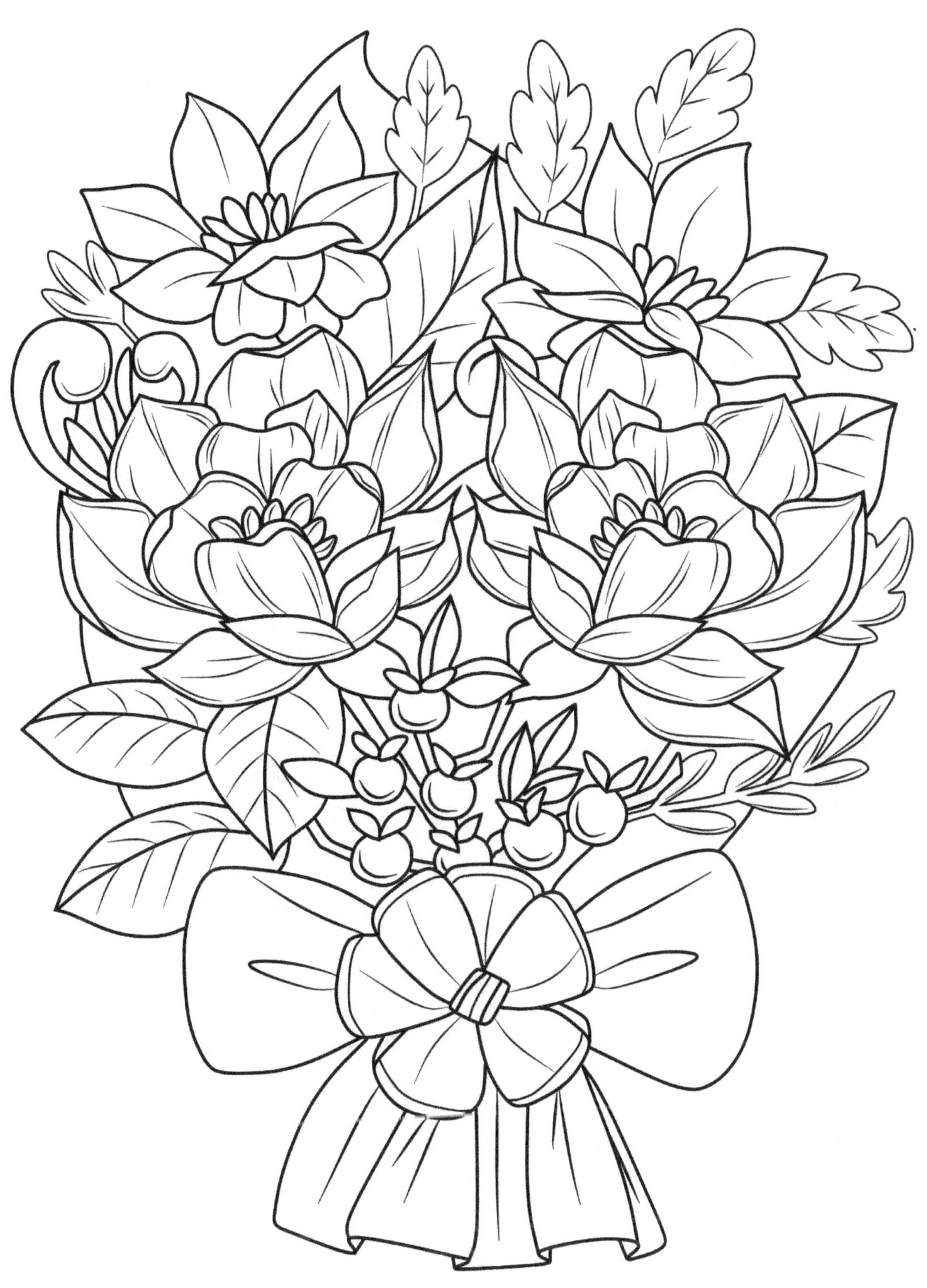

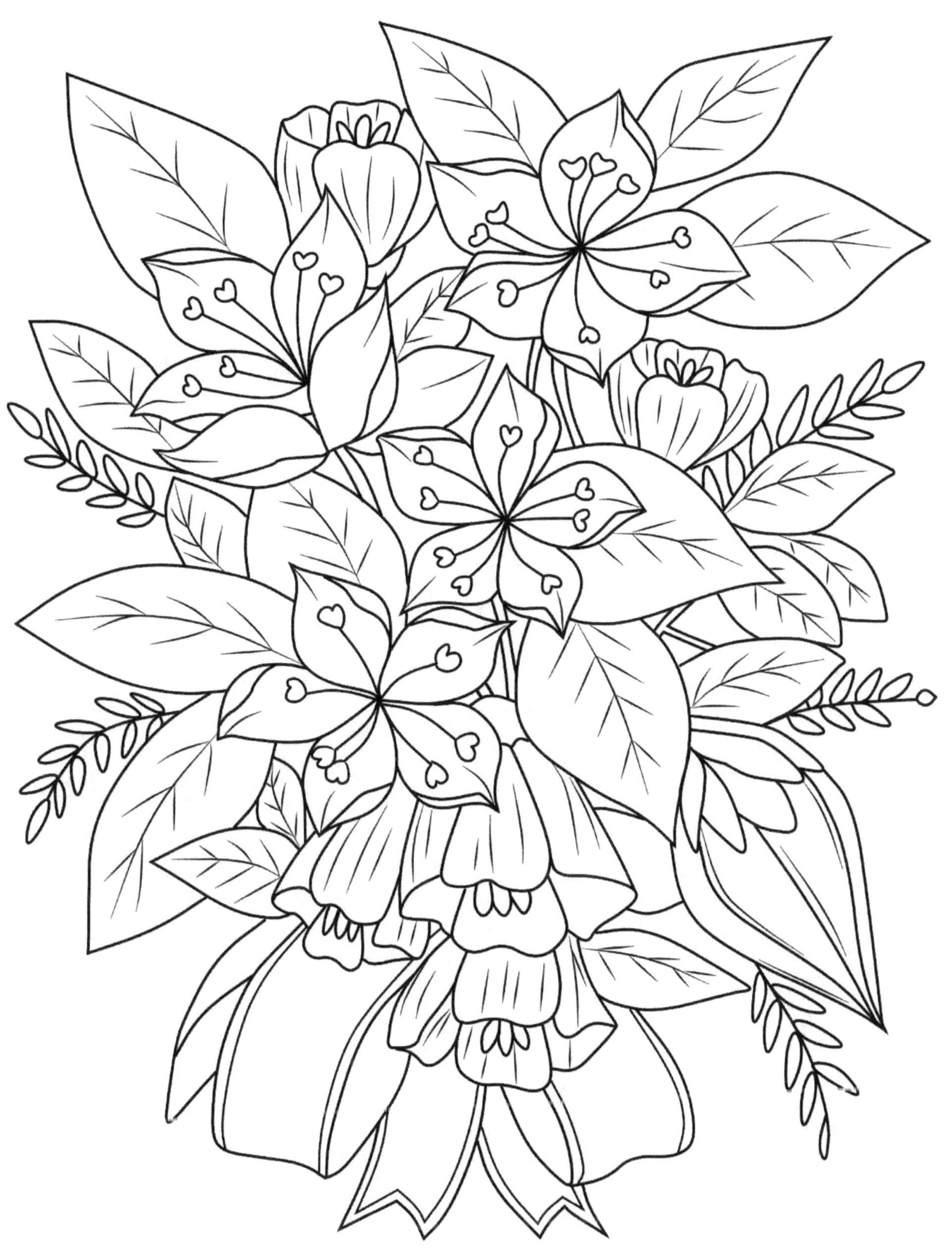

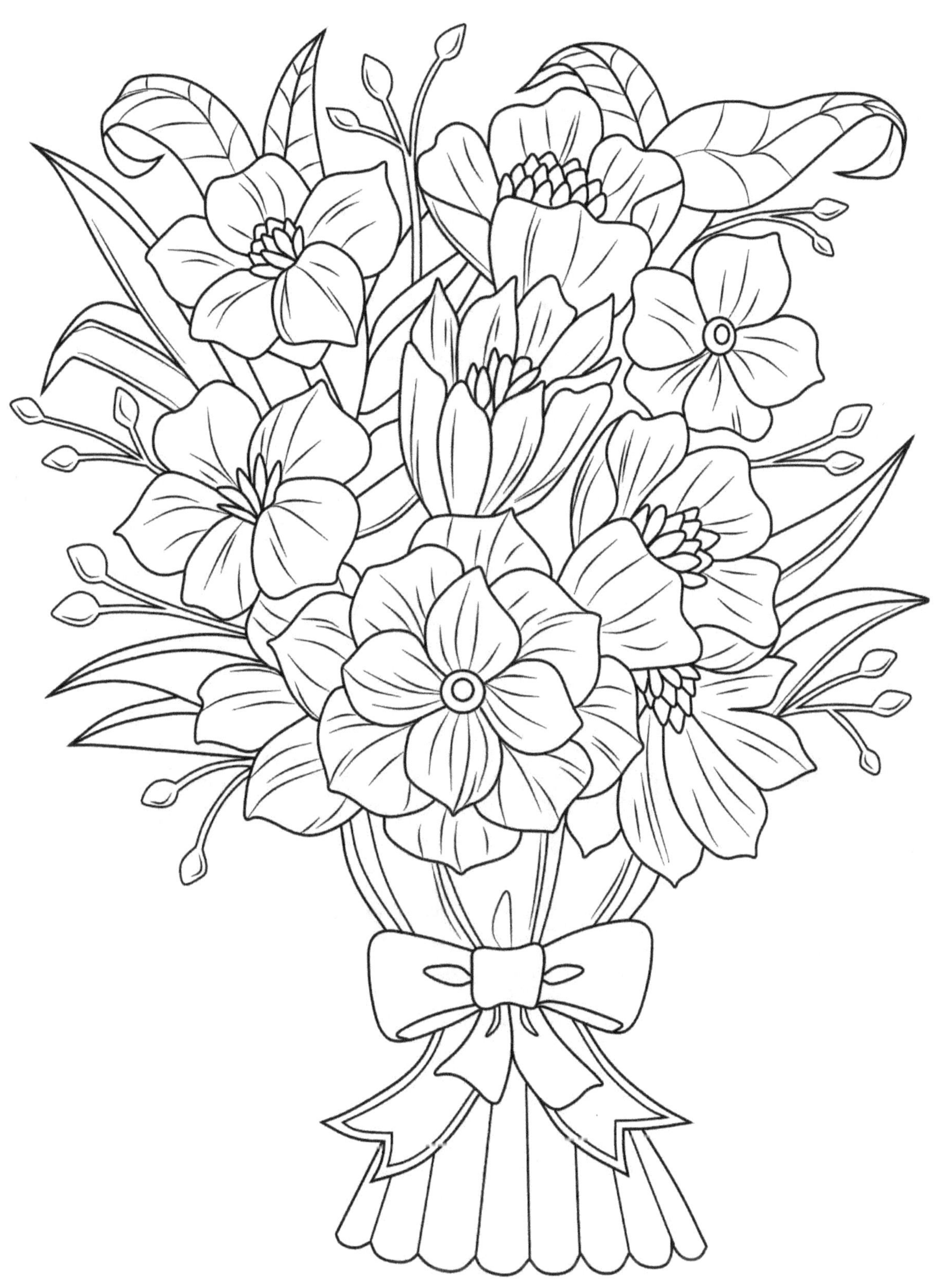

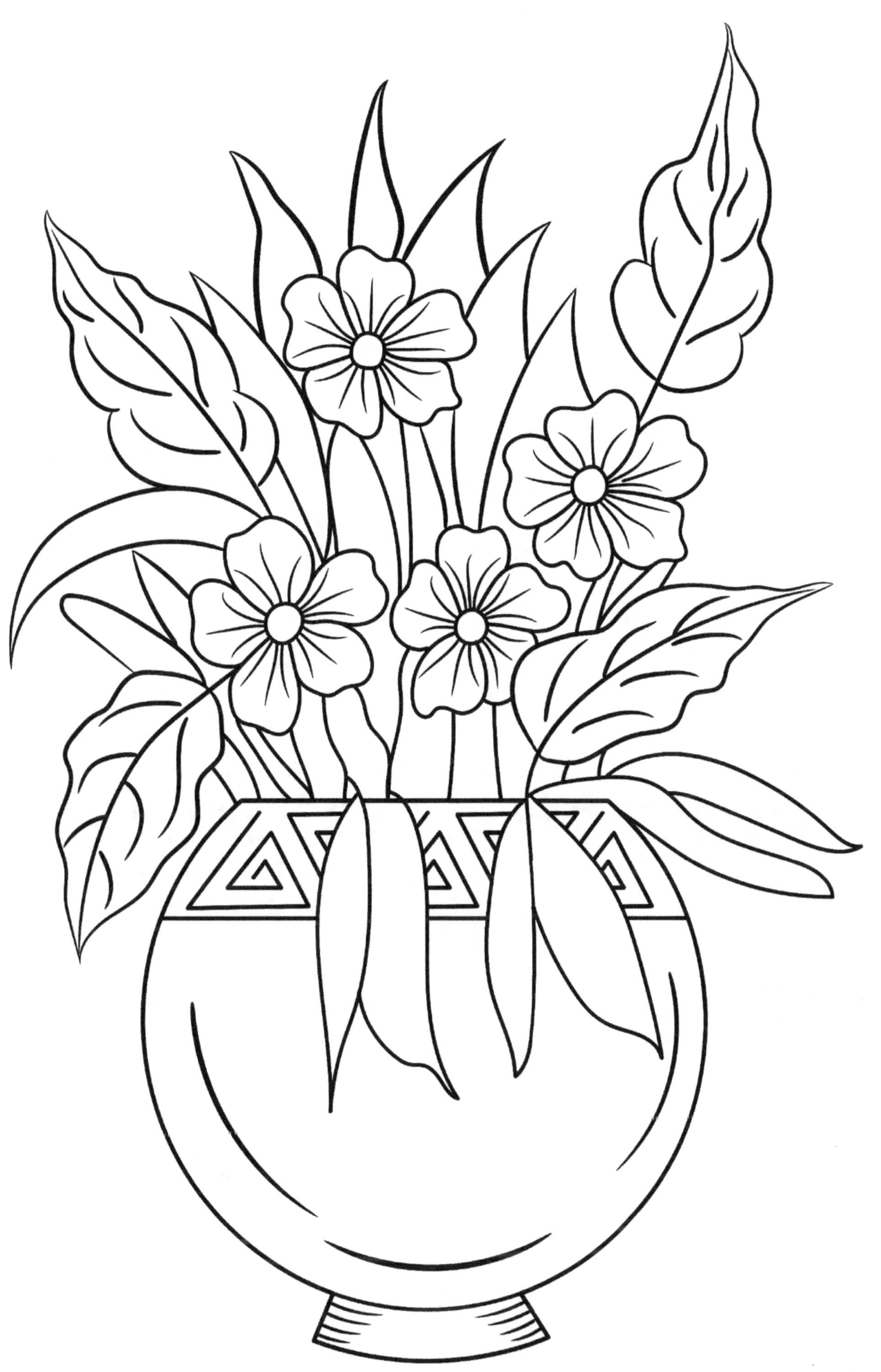

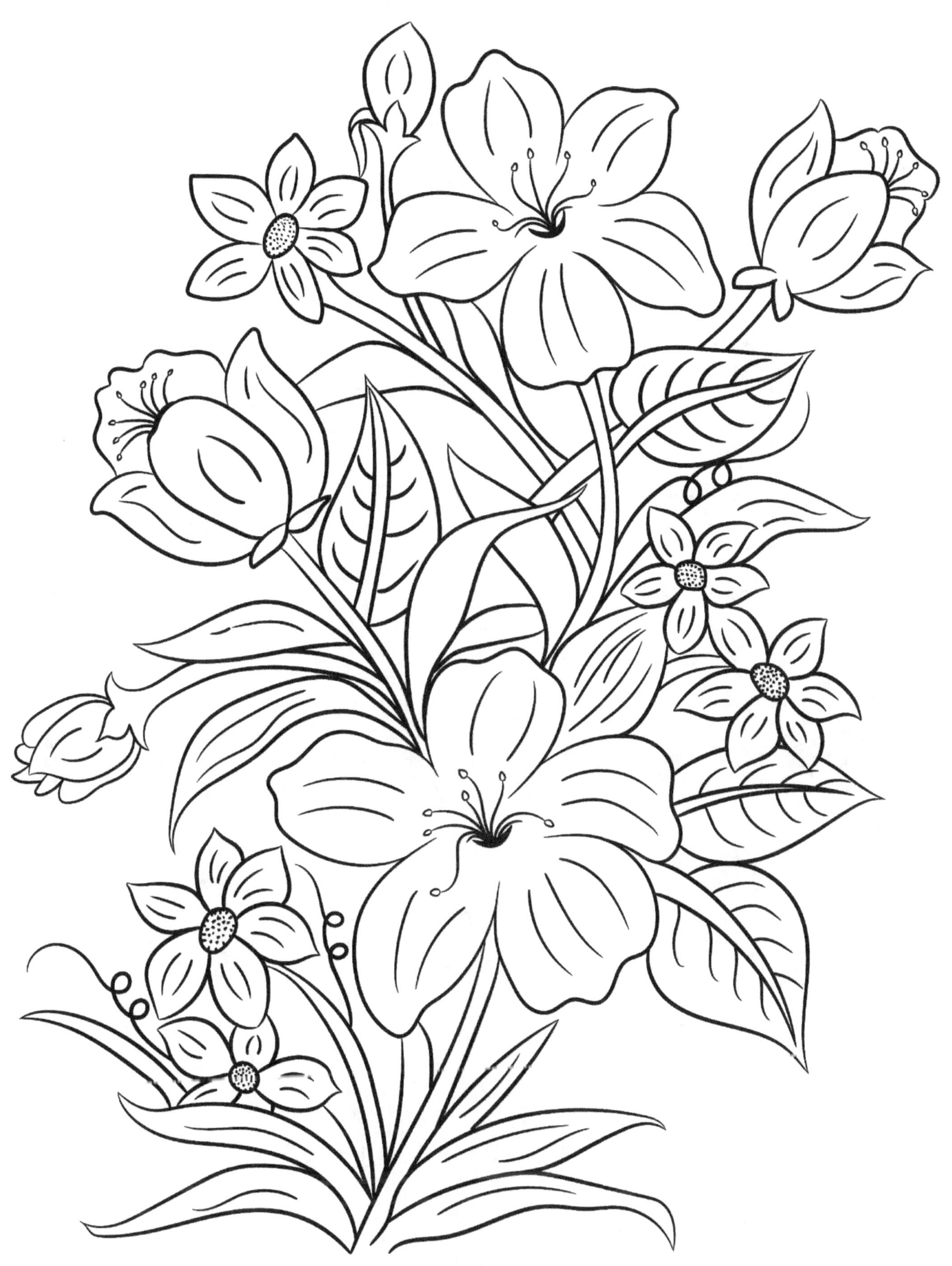

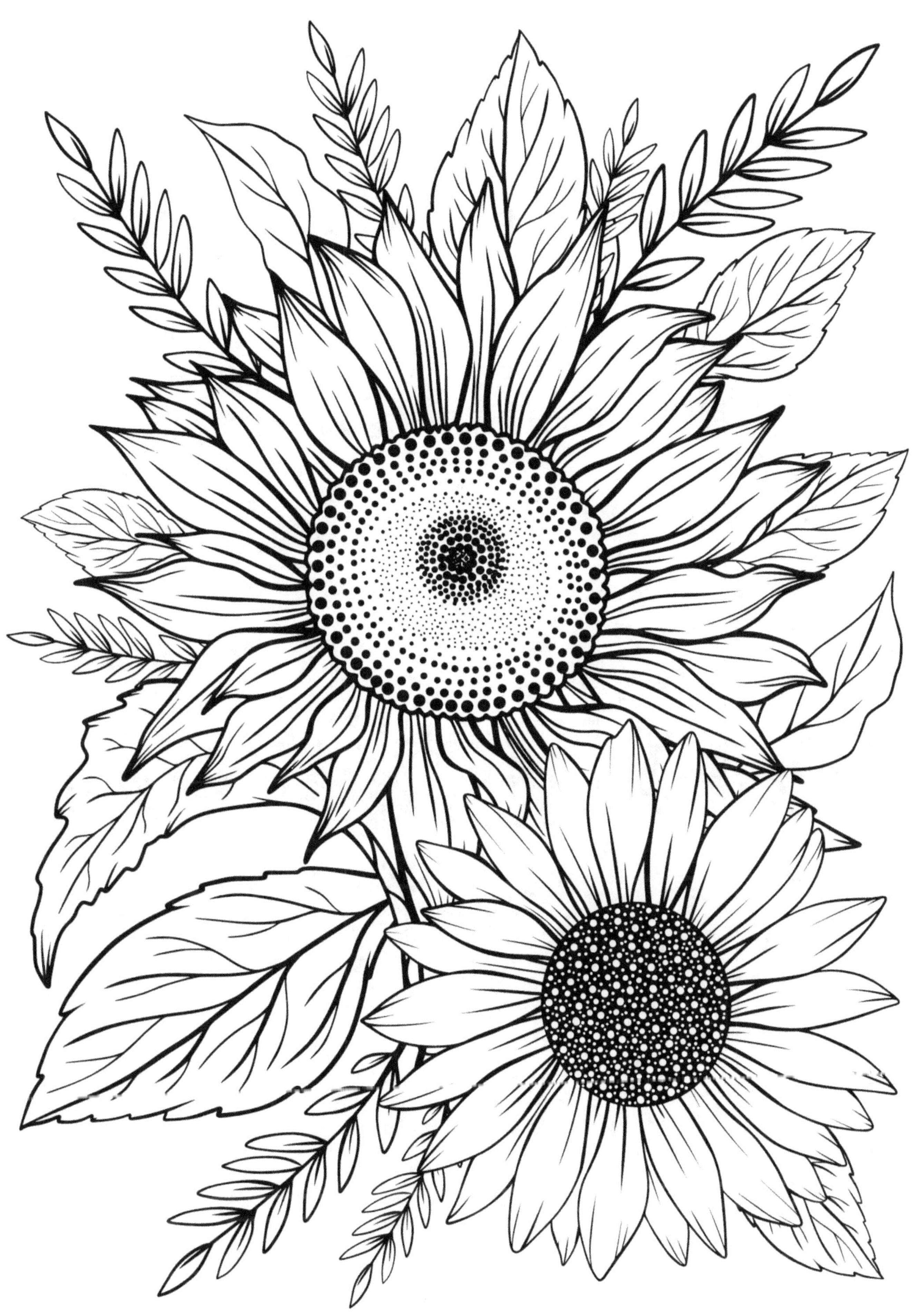

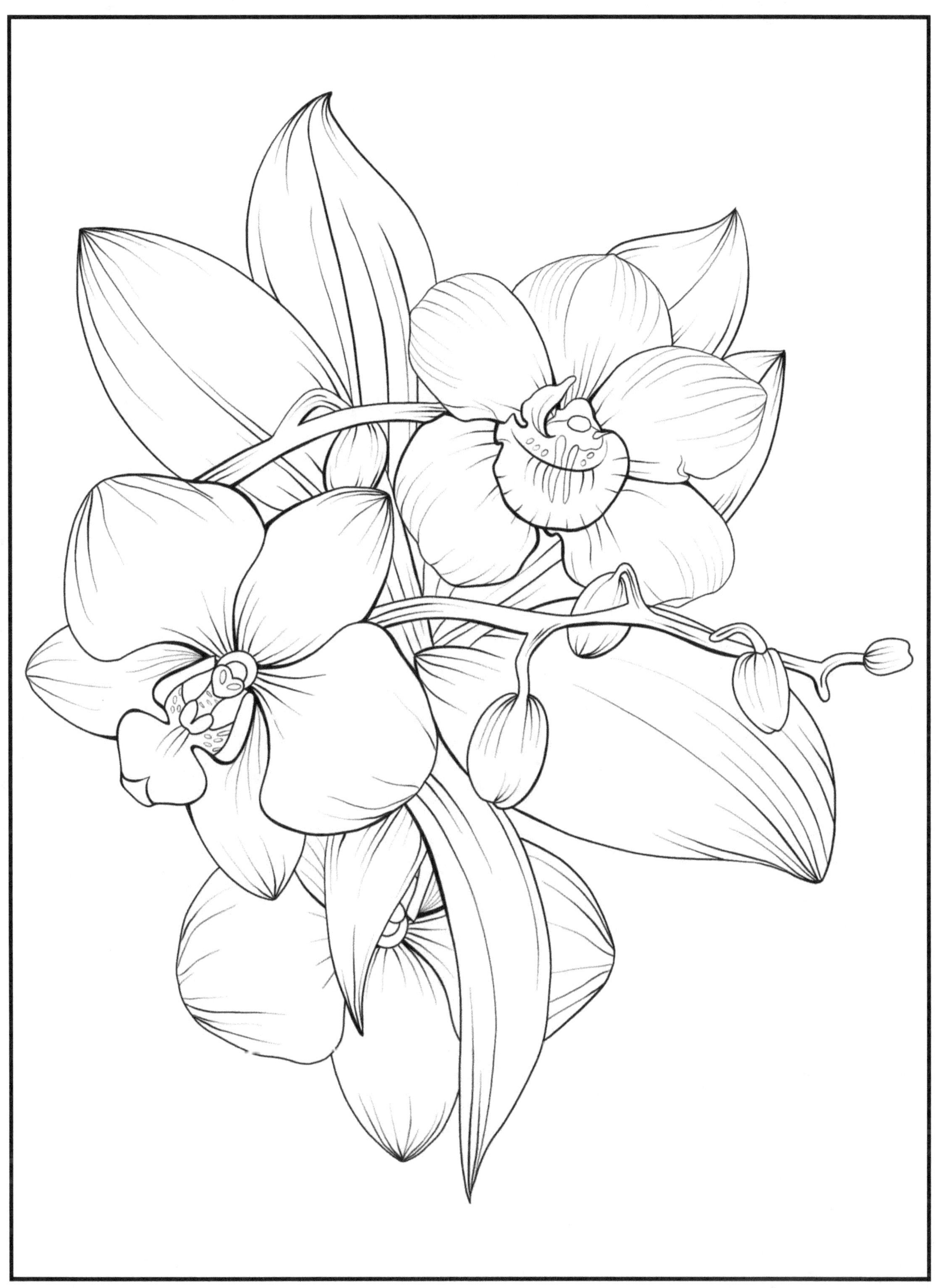

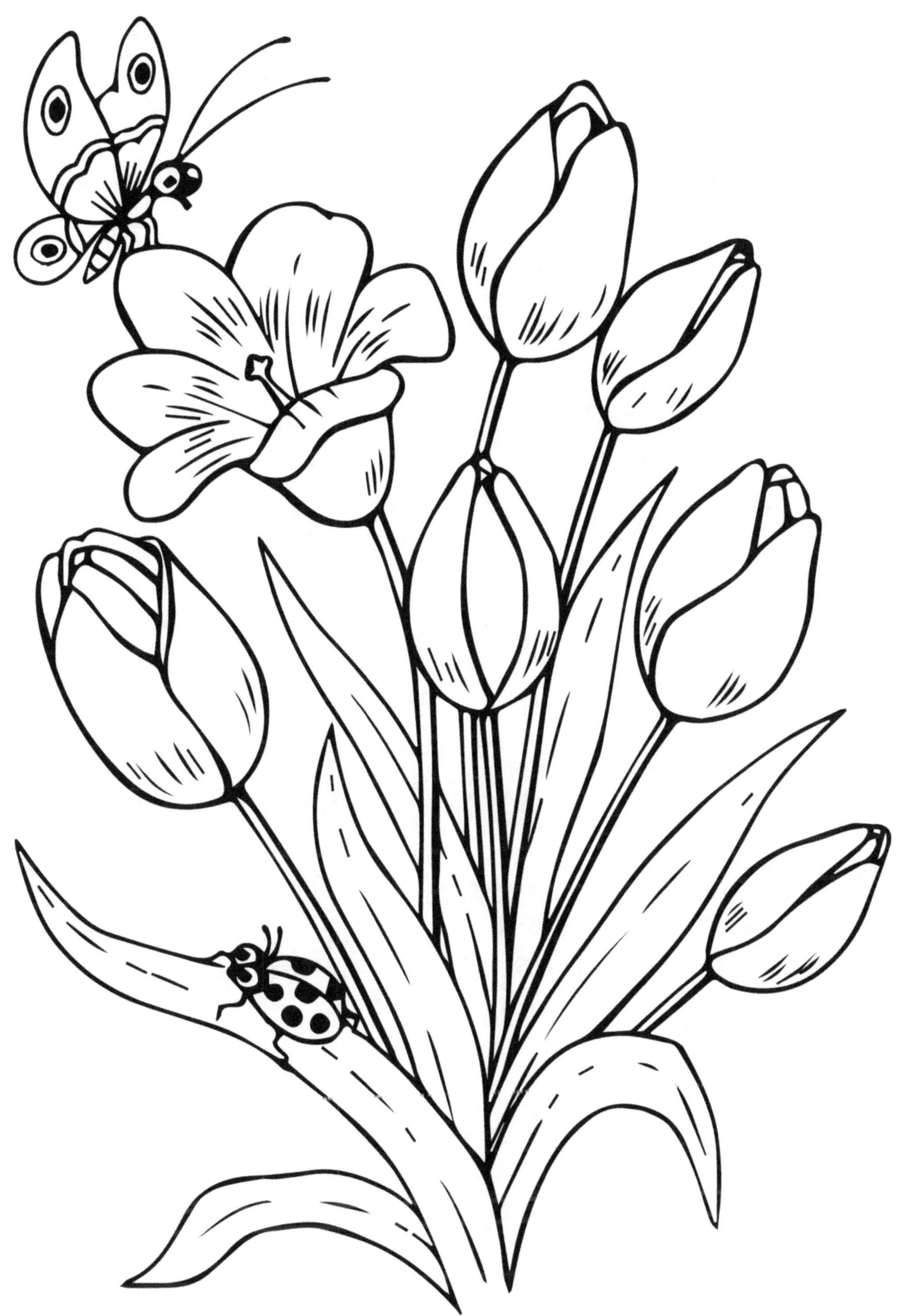

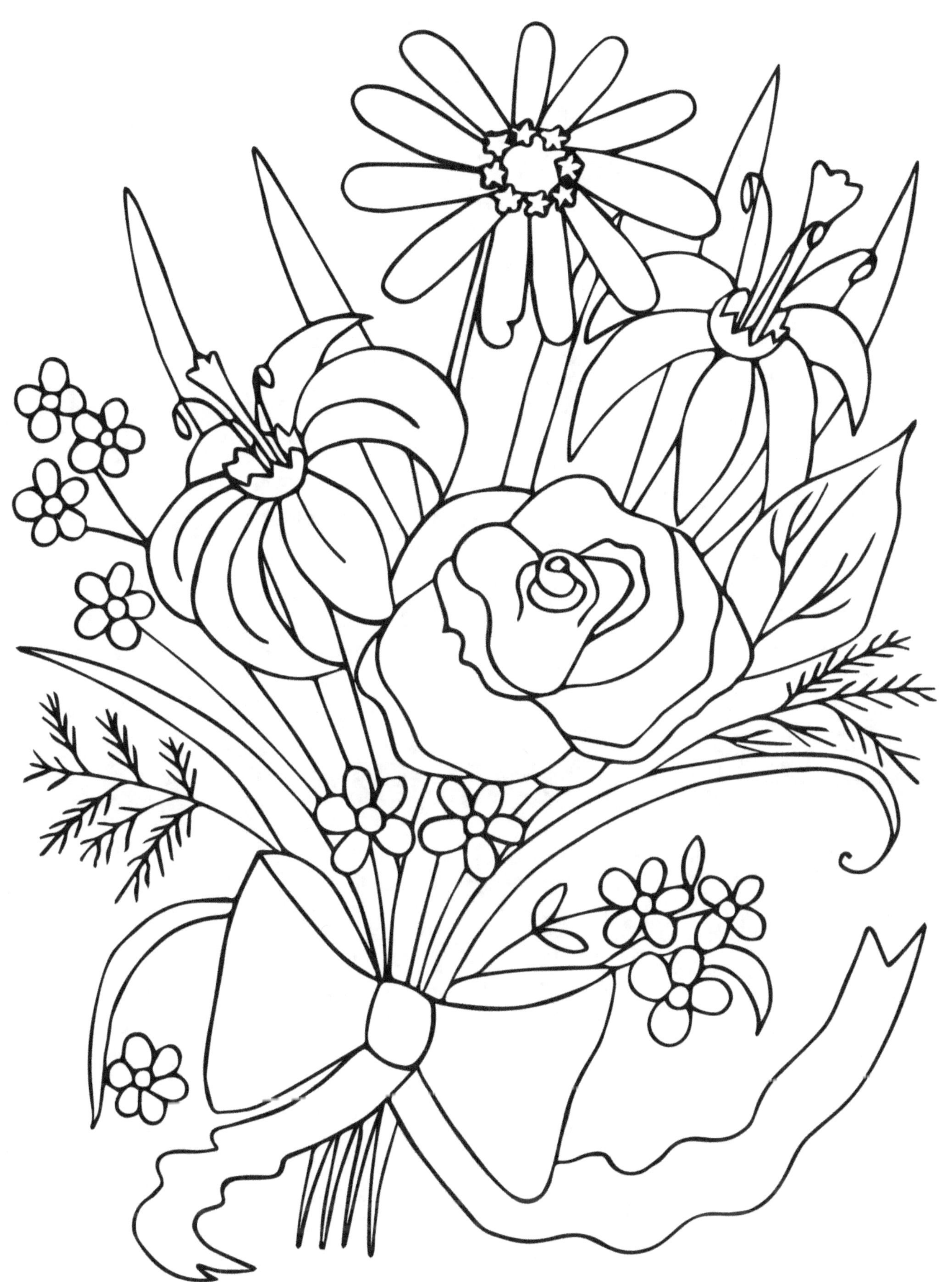

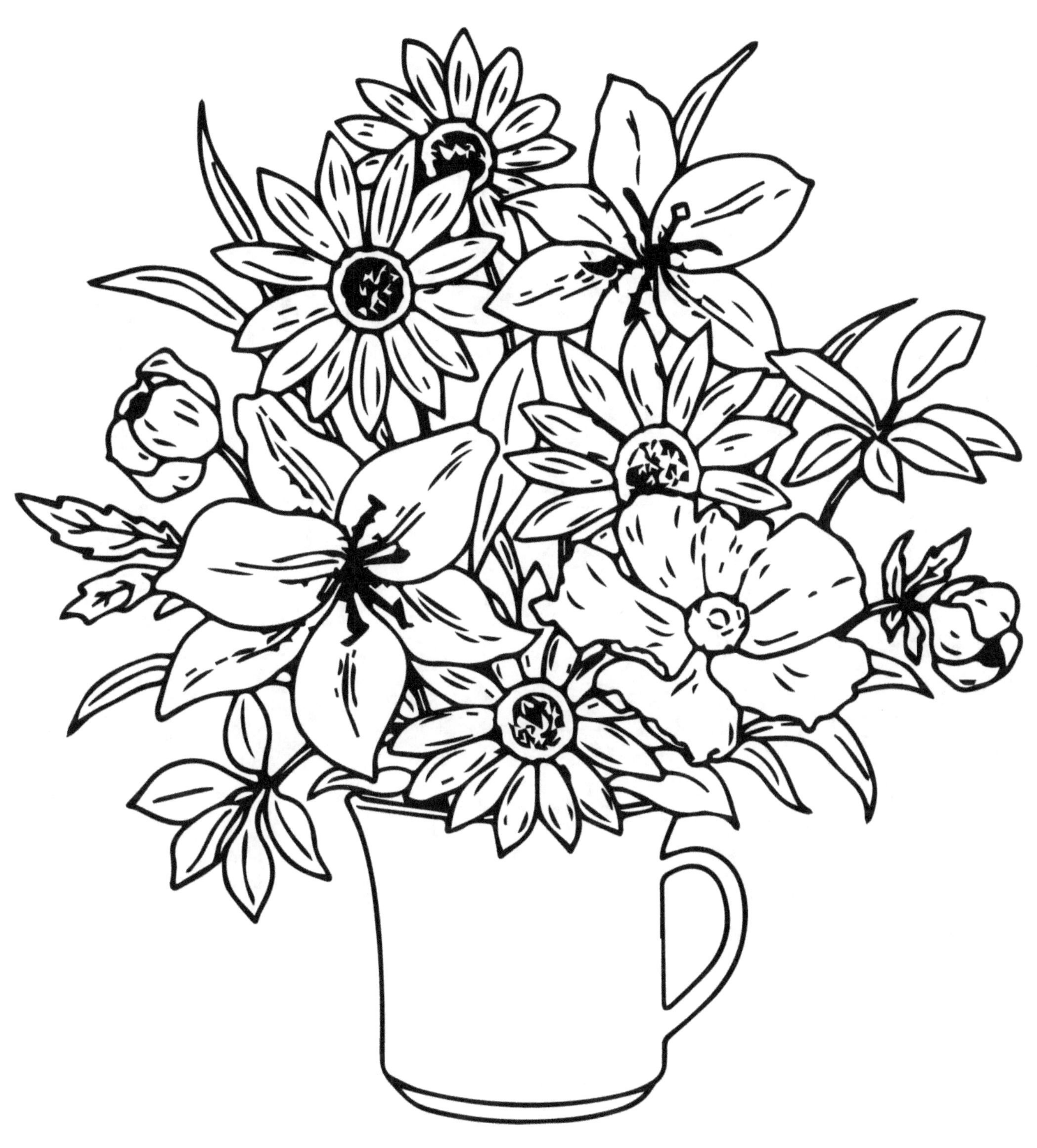

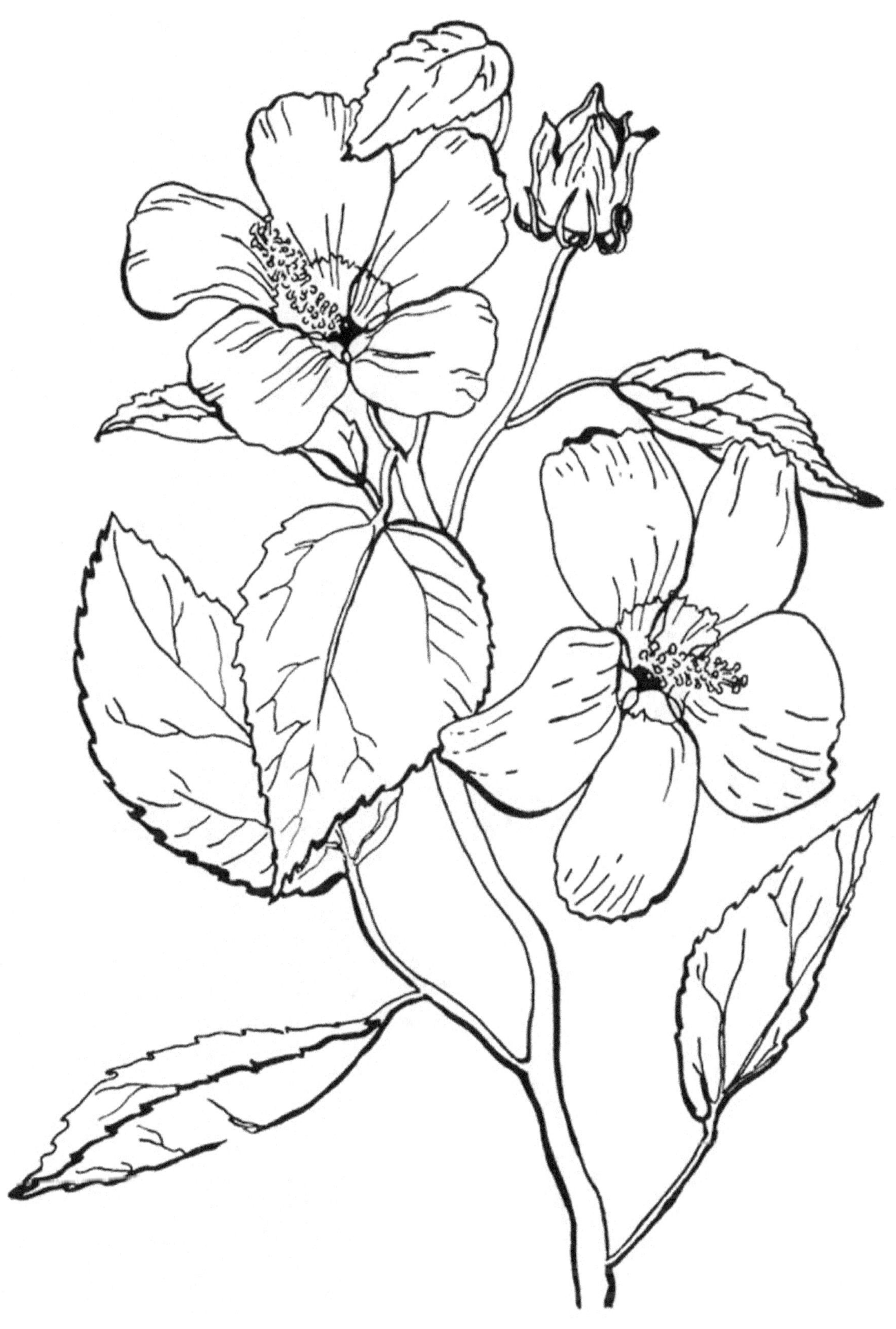

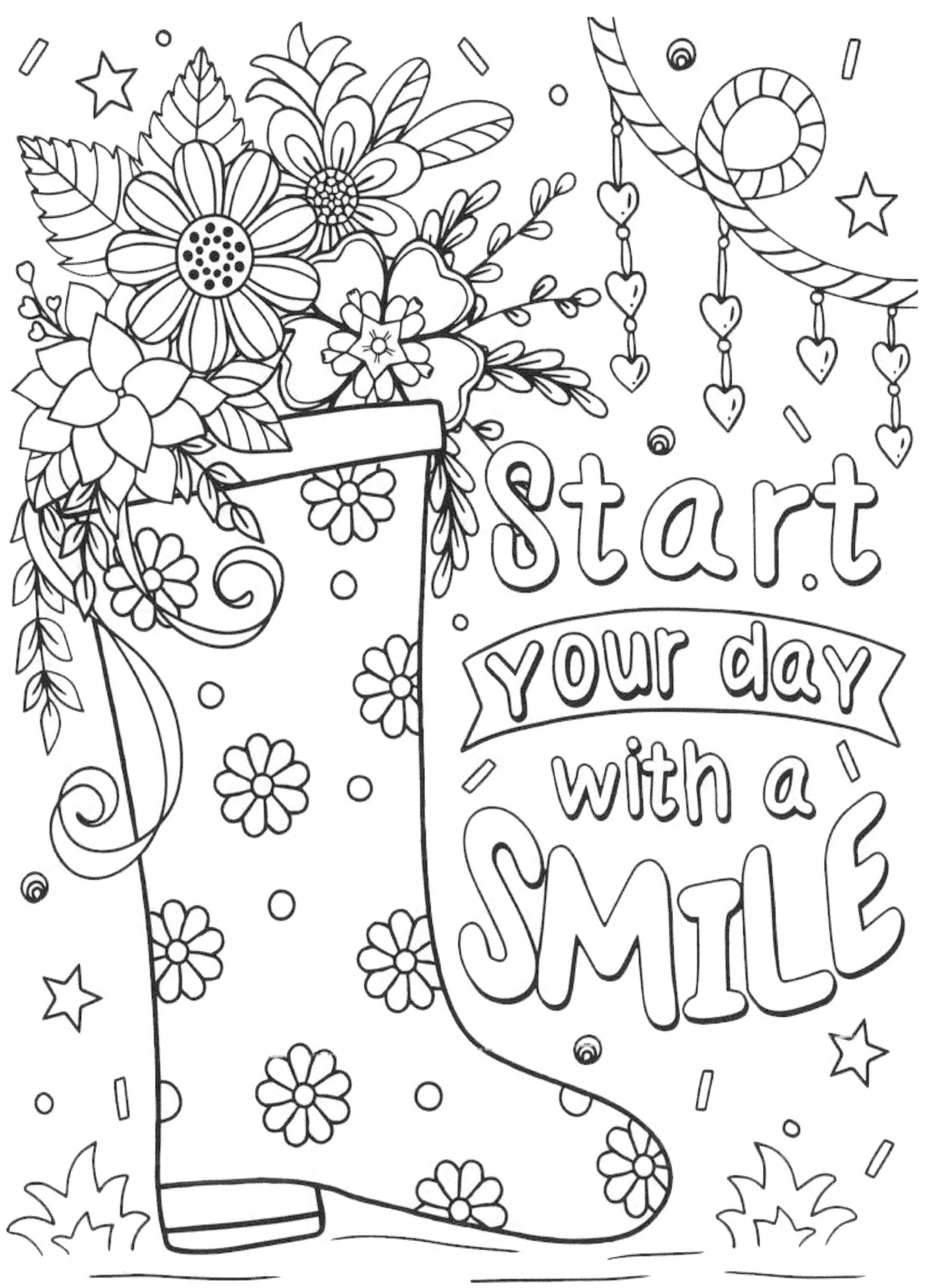

Start
your day
with a
SMILE

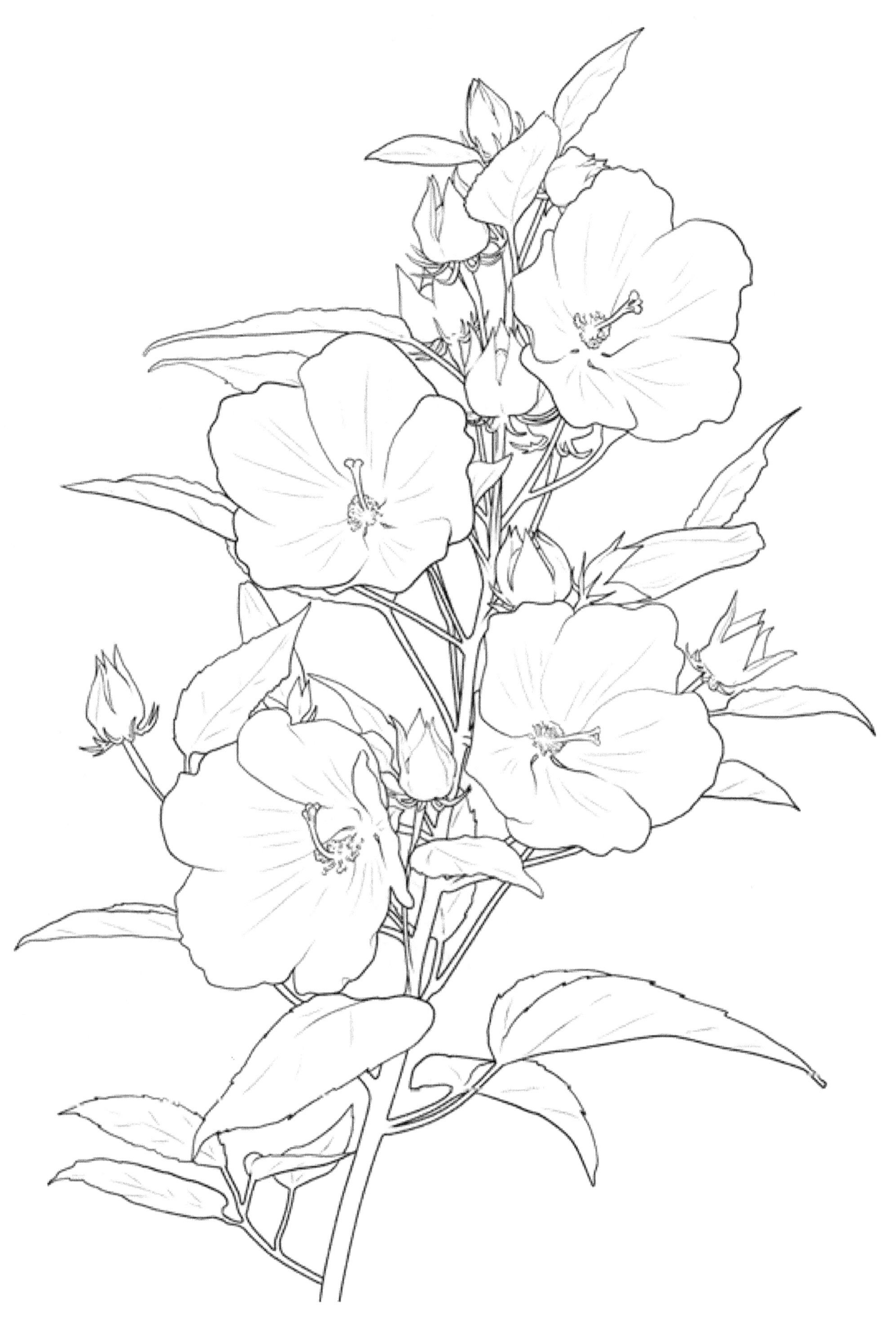

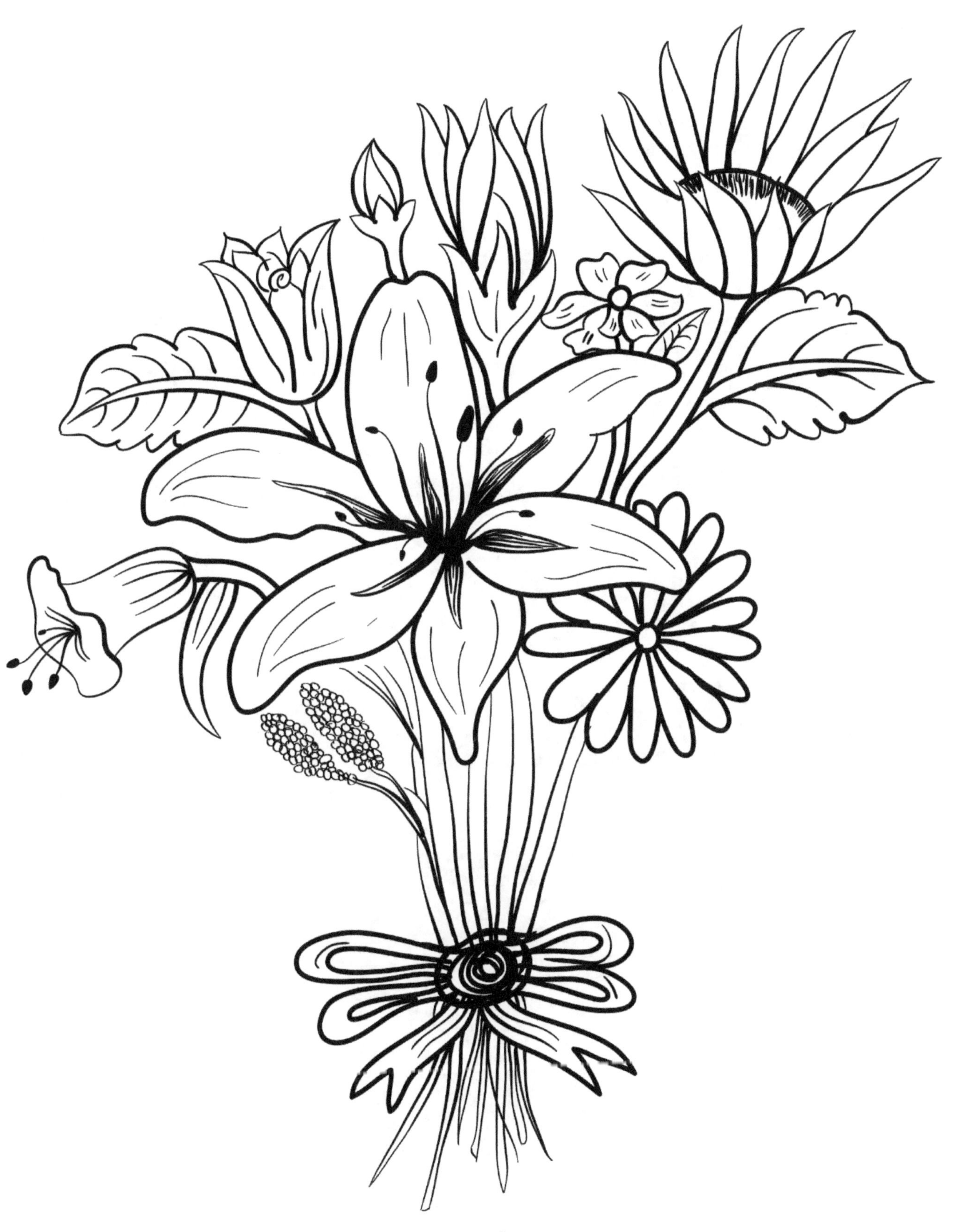

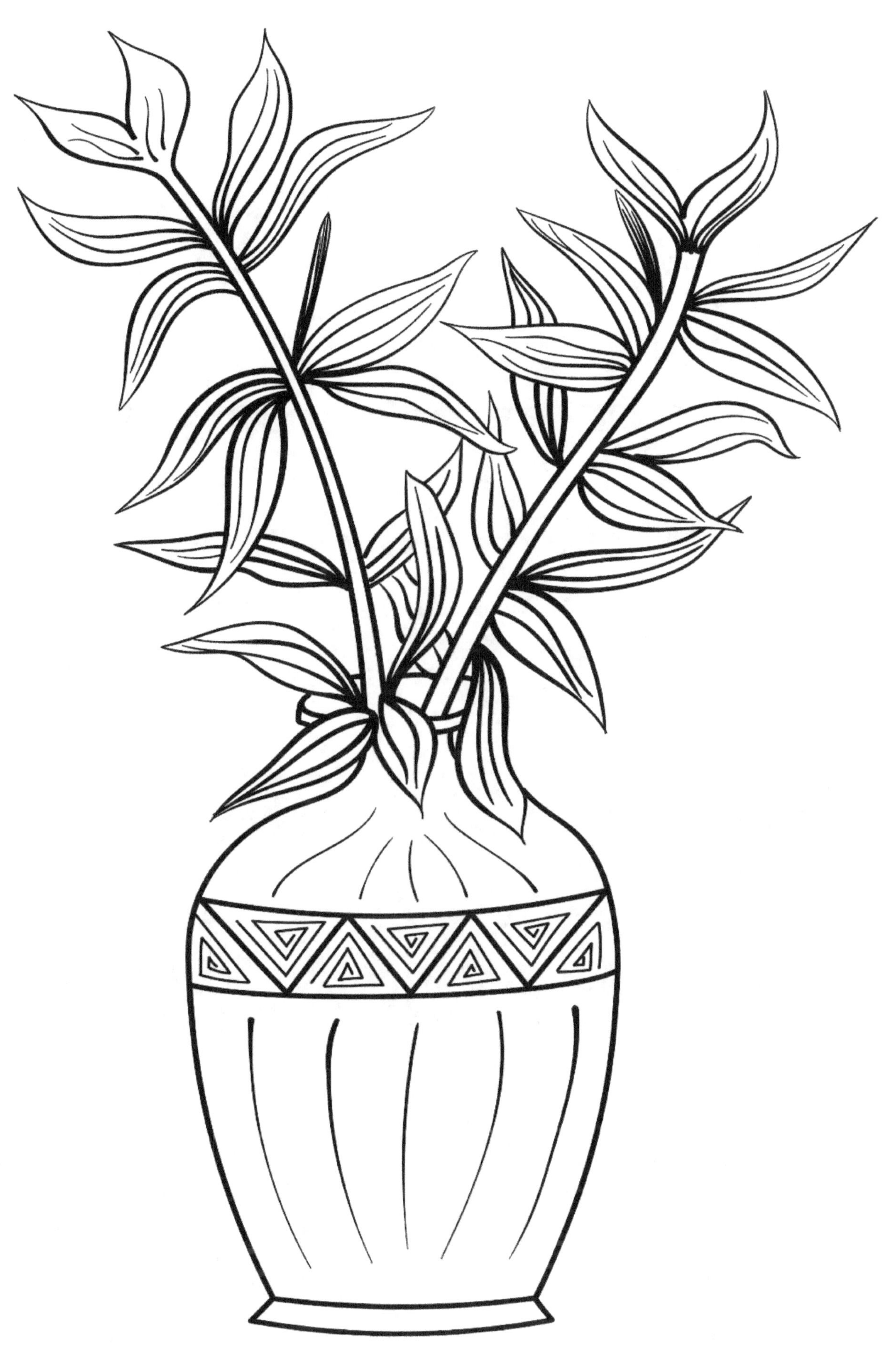